Hitler

Hitler

Alan Wykes

BB

Editor-in-Chief: Barrie Pitt
Editor: David Mason
Art Director: Sarah Kingham
Picture Editor: Robert Hunt
Designer: David Allen
Photographic Research: Nan Shuttleworth
Cartographer: Richard Natkiel

ISBN 0-345-24987-9-250

Manufactured in the United States of America

First Edition: March, 1971
Fifth Printing: April, 1976

Contents

6   Introduction

8   The victim

20   The man

32   The demagogue

50   The General

68   The General in action

94   The General in decline

124   The General in defeat

160   Bibliography

Der Führer

Introduction by Barrie Pitt

Not every reader will accept Alan Wykes' explanation of Hitler's behaviour as Party Leader and Dictator – which is that he had been infected in early manhood by syphilis and in later life succumbed to its tertiary effects: irrationality, irresponsibility and gross intemperance of speech and action. It is an explanation, nevertheless, which has been advanced before and to which the facts of his career will lend support. However, in the absence of documented evidence of this episode of his medical history – evidence which, as Alan Wykes makes clear, does not exist in a form which would stand up to judicial examination – the syphilis thesis must remain a thesis, albeit an arresting one.

Yet, the 'Vienna years', in which it is alleged Hitler contracted the disease, undoubtedly contain the key to much of his personality and destructive outlook. We now know that the story of a poverty stricken orphan's life which he propagated in *Mein Kampf* is largely a fabrication, and that the Austrian state, through the pension it paid him as the son of a civil servant, gave Hitler every chance to establish himself comfortably in life. He failed to do so because he squandered those means, and the dosshouse life to which he was reduced must accordingly be seen as one of his own choosing. For reasons all too readily understandable when the intensity of anti-Semitism in pre-war Vienna is recognised, Hitler blamed his lack of success and recognition principally on the Jews – not in any precisely formulated terms, for his mind never operated on precise lines, but in terms which laid upon the Jews responsibility for everything unpleasant, unjust and ill-organised

that he saw in the city and, by extension, experienced in his own life.

What roused Hitler from this self-imposed routine of emotional frustration and physical near-starvation was the Great War. He was intensely nationalistic (though not patriotic, of course, since he hated the Austrian Empire) and he eagerly accepted the chance this war offered him to cross the frontier and to join up in a German regiment. When the war ended, his record, his political outlook and ambitions and his very great natural talents were sufficient to launch him on the modest beginnings of a political career, under the sponsorship of the army. The relationship was to endure, though the army was to regret eventually that it had been entered into.

Hitler's relationships with individuals and with every organ and institution of German life have all been examined exhaustively. With none, however, was his relationship more critical than with the army. It gave him his start in politics and cast a protective cloak over his organis-

ation of the young Nazi party. It looked favourably on the Freikorps from which he drew so many of his earliest and most dedicated followers. But, as he was bitterly to discover, it would not brook attempts to seize power in the State without its specific approval. And hence it was bound to oppose Hitler's first attempt to make himself master of Germany – the Munich putsch of 1923. The lesson he learnt on 9th November, when his stormtroopers were shot down in the street by armed police, was one he never forgot: that in Germany, power belonged to whosoever commanded the army. Having failed to secure that command by force, Hitler spent the next few years securing it by ballot. Once attained, his earliest acts were directed to subordinating the army to his will and he did not rest in that aim until, in January 1942, he finally found the pretext to assume the office of Commander-in-Chief himself.

Given the obscurity of his background and hardships of his early life, it is hardly likely that Hitler could ever have felt much sympathy or liking for so unapologetically 'gentlemanly' a group as the German officer corps. Conflict between them was, indeed, inevitable, for their ideas on war were orthodox and Hitler's were not. Hence the shouting matches. The 'special effects' which went with the shouting – uncontrollable trembling, rolling of eyes and foaming at the mouth – might seem to lend support to the view that Hitler was the victim of chronic disease. However, those who knew Hitler from his Vienna days freely testify that such manifestations always accompanied his reactions to any persistent refutation of his views. He simply would not be contradicted, a habit which did not endear him to his comrades in the trenches later. It seems probable, therefore, that as Führer and Supreme Commander, when all outward constraints on his behaviour had been lifted, Hitler merely gave full rein to what was a natural trait. It always had its desired effect moreover. The generals blanched – and fell silent.

The victim

Those who set store by such things may care to know that the name Adolf derives from the two German words for 'noble wolf'. The family name Hitler is a variation of Hiedler and Hütler, both of which were borne by Adolf's forebears. Hiedler and Hütler have a tenuous association with the phrase 'guardian of the Gentiles' – which, considering Adolf's lifelong dedication to the hating and baiting of Jews, is not inappropriate, however fanciful.

There is unfortunately nothing fanciful about Adolf Hitler's existence. He began it on 20th April 1889 in a small hotel in Braunau, on the Austrian bank of the river Inn which divides Austria from Bavaria. Sixty-five miles to the west is Munich, the Bavarian capital, synonymous nowadays with the 'Peace in our time' conference at which the British Prime Minister, Neville Chamberlain, abjectly surrendered to Hitler on 29th September 1938. Sixty miles to the east is Linz, capital of Upper Austria, where Hitler went to school and ab-sorbed the pan-Germanic notions that nourished his fanatical xenophobia.

Adolf's father, Alois Hitler, had neither phobias nor philias. He was a minor civil servant, a clerk in the Customs and Excise department. He was a man of middle size with a head as round as a cabbage. He had out-handlebarred Hindenburg – at that time a famously fashionable young officer in the War Ministry – in the length of his moustaches and was harmlessly vain of his achievement. A conscientious worker, he had been undeservedly hapless in his domestic affairs. His first wife had died child-less; his second had died young leaving him two children to bring up; and his third – Adolf's mother – had given him four sons of whom three had died in infancy. Only Adolf and his sister Paula, plus the boy and girl of Alois' second marriage, had survived; and through the lens of hindsight one may

The infant Hitler. The first surviving picture, with newspaper announcement of his birth

8

J.F.Klinger   BRAUNAU
                               STADTGRABEN 318

The small hotel at Braunau in Austria where Hitler was born

have some harsh thoughts about fate's peculiar choices.

The Hitlers were Roman Catholics – though there is no evidence of special devoutness in the family – and Alois had to get a Papal Dispensation to marry Adolf's mother, Klara Pölzl, because her relationship to him of second cousin lay within the prohibited degrees of consanguinity. He was twenty-three years older than Klara when they were married in 1885; and when Adolf was six Alois retired from the Civil Service. In *Mein Kampf* Adolf says with characteristic pretentiousness that Alois 'bought a farm and tilled it himself'. What Alois in fact bought was a three-bedroomed house with a small garden in the village of Leonding, a mile or so from Linz. There he died in 1903.

Adolf Hitler was then fourteen and attending the secondary school in Linz. In *Mein Kampf* he is unforthcoming about his schooldays; and that is not surprising, for he could never bear to reveal anything about himself that didn't contribute something to a composite picture of genius and nobility. He was in fact no great shakes at anything at school. He had a mediocre talent for drawing and got an occasional grudging 'good' for his history and geography. But August Kubizek, who was his contemporary and who wrote a book *The Young Hitler*, says that he was idle and unstable by nature, though 'he really loved his mother. I swear to it before God and man. I remember many occasions when he showed this love for his mother most deeply and movingly during her last illness [she died of cancer in 1908]; he never spoke of his mother but with deep affection. He was a good son . . . he always carried his mother's portrait with him'.

Adolf was also affectionately inclined toward a girl called discreetly by Kubizek 'Stefanie'. If we are to believe Kubizek, Hitler was Stefanie's love-lorn swain. She was considerably above his social station and used to drive daily along the Linz promenade in a carriage with her mother. Hitler stood on the sidewalk with his friends and tried to ogle her. But 'from time to time the two ladies were to be seen in the company of young officers. Poor, pallid youngsters like Adolf naturally could not hope to cope with these young lieutenants in their smart uniforms . . . his anger, in the end, led him into uncompromising enmity toward the officer class as a whole, and everything military in general. "Conceited blockheads", he used to call them. It annoyed him intensely that Stefanie mixed with such idlers who, he insisted, wore corsets and used scent.'

He wrote countless love poems to Stefanie, Kubizek tells us, and goes on to describe one of them in which 'a high-born damsel (none other than Stefanie) in a dark blue flowing gown, rode on a white steed over the flowering meadows, her loose hair falling in golden waves over her shoulders. A clear spring sky was above. Everything was pure radiant joy. I can still see Adolf's face glowing with fervent ecstasy and hear his voice reciting those verses. Stefanie filled his thoughts so completely that everything he said, or did, or planned for the future, was centred round her. With his growing estrangement from his home, Stefanie gained more and more influence over my friend, although he never spoke a word to her'.

Hitler's estrangement from his home was caused by Alois's determination to have his son enter the Civil Service and Adolf's equal determination to become a painter – which was, for him, a way of saying he didn't want to work. His tiny talent for drawing had become greatly inflated in his own mind. He says in *Mein Kampf* that when he boldly told his father what he wanted to do Alois replied, 'Artist! Not as long as I live, never!' Looking at Hitler's vapid water colours, which are of about the same value to visual art as is *In a Monastery Garden* to music, one can't help feeling that Alois' indignant discouragement was a good thing, though it was a social indignation rather than an aesthetic one.

The estrangement became translated into terms of actual separation after Alois died, but not for several years. Adolf was too stupid and too idle to pass his school-leaving examination and his mother kept him cosseted at home until she too died.

He had attempted to enter the Vienna Academy of Fine Arts but was unable to pass the entrance examination. 'Test drawing unsatisfactory', the Classifications List of 1907 says curtly. He tried again a year later and was again turned down. Indignantly he ranted about 'injustice' and forced an interview with the Vice-chancellor. He got short shrift there, being told merely to try the School of Architecture since his drawings showed marginally more talent in that direction. But the School of Architecture refused his application because he had no School Leaving Certificate.

Thus he was left high and dry with no hope of becoming what he doubtless saw himself to be – the Austrian Michelangelo. In place of that lofty achievement he developed a grudge against the Academy's 'system'. It was the first of many grudges that he was to brood upon.

Bereft now of his mother, whose indulgent cosseting had been like balm on the wounds of his frustration, he set off for Vienna, his self-pity turned inside out so that he saw himself as a conquering hero.

'With my clothes and linen packed in a valise and with an indomitable resolution in my heart, I left for Vienna. I hoped to forestall fate, as my father had done some fifty years before. I was determined to become "something",

Hitler's parents. *Left:* Alois Hitler, a minor customs official. *Above:* His third wife, Klara Pölzl

but certainly not a civil servant.'

He became, as we know, a conqueror of a sort – the bullying sort – and to millions of the German people a hero too; but for the time being he was nothing but a roustabout – ill-clad, ill-fed, and forced to live on such wits as he had. Rheinhold Hanisch, another roustabout who knew him in Vienna, says that he wore an ancient black overcoat (a gift from a Jew named Neumann) which reached below his knees, that his hair hung long over his collar from under a greasy black bowler hat, and that his thin face was covered with a black beard. 'Years of study and suffering in Vienna' is the title of the relevant chapter in *Mein Kampf*, but Hitler omits to mention that his study was limited to rehashing other men's ideas or that his suffering was caused by his own idleness.

Neumann the Jew, Hanisch, a man called Siegfried Loffner, and two others appearing here as Stefan and Daniel because at the time of writing they are still alive and, for reasons that will appear in a moment, entitled to the privacy of pseudonyms, have all confirmed that Hitler lived as they did. They carried luggage, beat carpets, called cabs, washed dishes and scavenged round dustbins. Neumann and Hanisch acted as his 'art agents' for a time, accompanying him to shops and sometimes persuading the proprietors to commission posters and price tickets which Hitler would do on the spot; or persuading picture framers to put his sugary water colours in their windows where they occasionally sold to people who liked such things. (Hanisch's kindness was repaid by Hitler taking legal action against him for the embezzlement of part of a sum Hanisch got for a picture; and Hanisch was sent to prison for a week, the case having been proved.) That was the extent of Hitler's 'study and suffering' in Vienna. He had a great distaste for regular work, preferring to earn a little money and spend it frugally in cafés where he read newspapers and harangued the customers on politics.

He was a great bore with his continual sounding-off about injustices and inefficiencies in 'the system', his spouting of half digested information from indiscriminate reading, and his dotty ideas for acquiring fame. And like most manic-depressives he was always either sullen or exuberant, shattering everyone's peace with rantings against Jews, Habsburgs, Catholics or Social Democrats, or withdrawing into himself and refusing to say anything to anybody. He was a self-confessed cheat even before he left Linz. He told Hanisch that he had many times faked 'old masters' by painting pictures in oils and baking them in the oven so that they turned yellow and apparently ancient. And with considerable practice in cheap oratory he learned to cheat with words too, so that sloppy platitudes could be so spiced with paranoiac bitterness that they sounded like the trumpetings of a saviour of the German race.

The 'years of study and suffering in

13

Vienna' amounted in all to four. In 1913 he took himself off to Munich, where he hoped to fare better. But meanwhile something of great importance happened.

The lodgings, dosshouses, crypts, halls, cafés, parks and churches where Hitler stayed in Vienna are innumerable and for the most part untraceable. But one of them, at 27 Meldemannstrasse, is without doubt one of the places where the would-be saviour of the German race laid his weary head. It was situated in the XXth (northeast) District of the city, near the Danube, and it was euphemistically known as a 'Men's Home' though its status was no more than that of a dosshouse. The pseudonymous Stefan and Daniel stayed there with him; and it is from their testimony, made years later to the London venereologist Dr T Anwyl-Davies, that one can establish the facts.

Both Stefan and Daniel remember a bitter quarrel on an evening in April 1910. The quarrel was over a girl, a Jewish whore named Hannah, and it was caused by Hitler's having appropriated her to his own use when she was being paid by the others. Since Hitler was already indebted to Stefan and Daniel for such hospitality as their circumstances allowed, there was every justification for their reproach; and they were by no means reluctant to shower it upon him. They followed their home-truths with a good beating up. They pushed him into the dormitory, bashed him over the head and in the ribs, and flung him into the street. He screamed imprecations at them and by way of reply they flung his inks, pens, paints and brushes after him. That was the last they saw of him that night.

After an hour or so they both went out again, this time to find Hannah and bring her in from her beat. Her trade was mostly in doorways near the Nordwestbahnhof – a rapid but wearying trade sometimes involving four customers an hour (at fifty heller each, that is about threepence by

1910 values) and she no doubt found the dosshouse, with its lousy biscuit beds, comparatively comfortable and her customers Stefan and Daniel comparatively undemanding. They recall that she often stayed an hour or two (having bribed the janitor, who was the only person concerned with the No Women rule, with a few cigarettes on the way in) and then returned to her beat near the station.

On this particular evening they noticed that the faint rash they had seen on her body on the last occasion they had been with her had disappeared. She could hardly be called clean, but at least she no longer looked as if she had what they had thought might be heat rash or flea bites in the fading-out stage. It may seem naïve for two young men in their late teens and obviously promiscuous to suppose anything so innocent as flea bites on their consort; but although they had heard of venereal diseases their knowledge was vague. It certainly included nothing about the diseases' clinical manifestations; and even if it had they were living – existing, rather – in a manner that would have left them indifferent. If they had known on that evening that they were already incubating in their bodies the germs of syphilis transferred from Hannah on the occasion of their previous intercourse they would have been maliciously heartened to know too that Hitler also had been corrupted – and on the very occasion for which they had been lambasting him. Knowing nothing, they satisfied themselves in turn with Hannah, gave her the hundred heller or so they could scrape up between them, and turned her loose.

Hitler returned to lodge at the dosshouse a week or two later. Stefan and Daniel took no exception to that: they had worked their indignation off by beating him up and couldn't be bothered to extend their enmity. But they observed that when he took off his clothes to have them de-loused by baking in the dosshouse oven, he, like

themselves, had a suspicion of a pink rash. They still didn't associate the rash with Hannah; nor did their general feeling of ill-being seem to them remarkable. They were not living the kind of life likely to encourage hundred per cent health; and when, after a while, the rash was accompanied by various other unpleasant manifestations they wisely went to a doctor, and on being told the alarming diagnosis of syphilis were maliciously comforted when they recalled that Hitler had exhibited the same rash. By now he was probably in the same unpleasant state that they were in. They accepted the treatment the doctor was able to give them, which at that time was an ointment compounded mainly of mercury, and wondered if Hitler too had had the sense to seek medical aid.

It seems to all intents and purposes certain that he did not - anyway not at that early stage of infection when treatment is vital. Felix Kersten, personal physician to Heinrich

Adolf Hitler (back row, middle) and classmates at primary school. Despite the confident pose, his school career was undistinguished

Himmler, the Gestapo chief, offers the soundest evidence that Hitler was irrevocably gripped by the disease. In his diary for 12th December 1942 he writes:

'This was the most exciting day I've had since I first began treating Himmler. (Kersten was a therapist who was able to relieve Himmler of pain caused by an internal illness.) He was very nervous and restless; I realized that he had something on his mind and questioned him about it. His reply was to ask me: "Can you treat a man suffering from severe headaches, dizziness and insomnia?"

'"Of course, but I must examine him before I can give a definite opinion," I answered. "Above all I must know the cause of these symptoms."

'Himmler replied: "I'll tell you who he is. But you must swear to tell no-

15

By 1944 Hitler was heavily dependent on the drugs and quackish remedies of Dr Morell, his personal physician

body about it and treat what I confide in you with the utmost secrecy."

'My answer was; that as a doctor, I was constantly having secrets entrusted to me; it was no new experience for me, as the strictest discretion was part of my professional duty.

'Himmler then fetched a black portfolio from his safe and took a blue manuscript from it, saying: "Read this. Here are the secret documents with the report on the Führer's illness."

'The report comprised twenty-six pages and at a first glance I realized that it had drawn freely on Hitler's medical record from the days when he lay blinded in a hospital at Pasewalk. From there the report went on to establish that in his youth as a soldier Hitler had fallen a victim to poison gas; he had been incompetently treated so that for a time he was in danger of blindness. There were also, even in that early report, symptoms associated with syphilis. In 1937 symptoms appeared which proved that syphilis was continuing its ravages; and at the beginning of 1942 symptoms of a similar nature showed beyond any shadow of doubt that Hitler was suffering from progressive paralysis. Every symptom was present except for fixity of vision and confusion of speech.

'I handed the report back to Himmler and informed him that unfortunately I could do nothing in this case as my speciality was manual therapy, not venereal disease.

'He told me that Morell (Hitler's personal physician) was giving him injections and asserted that they would check the progress of the disease, and in any event maintain the Führer's ability to work.'

There is a good deal of more conjectural evidence of Hitler's syphilitic state. The fact that 'Professor' Theodore Morell, the quack doctor who cunningly installed himself as the Führer's personal physician, had originally come to the Hitler *ménage* to treat Heinrich Hoffman, Hitler's photographer, for venereal infection is not without significance. Nor is the fact that Helmut Spiethoff, a venereologist of renown, was appointed to Hitler's contingent of medicos in the early 1930s and the records of his consultations seized and impounded by the Nazi leader Wilhelm Frick when Hitler became *Reichskanzler*. And both Heinz Linge, his valet, and Karl Brandt, surgeon to his staff, have described symptoms typical of syphilis in an advanced stage – maniacal ravings, palsy of the limbs, acute hypochondria, continual itching of the skin, insomnia, and pains in the head and stomach.

But it is the testimony of those two men Stefan and Daniel, given to Anwyl-Davies, whose reputation as a venereologist could not be higher, that comes closest to proof that Hitler caught the disease in 1910. And the secret report shown by Himmler to Kersten can hardly be denied as evidence that its ravages continued. The syphilis germ, *Spirochaeta pallida*, can attack every organ in the body and Hitler's final ravings are an almost certain indication that the cortex of his brain had been attacked, making general paralysis of the insane inevitable.

The possibility of Hitler's syphilitic state and its effect on his character and conduct has of course been considered before, though without the supporting evidence of his fellow victims. But there has been considerable reluctance to accept the fact that he was infected – though for no understandable reason. The social stigma still lingering round venereal diseases could scarcely have influenced the thinking of the enemies of a man like Hitler. Better men than him have become infected with syphilis –

Gauguin and Schumann for example – or – like Beethoven – inherited it, and no one has batted an eyelid over its effect upon their nature and work. But even such a distinguished biographer as Alan Bullock (in his *Hitler: a Study in Tyranny*) says that 'such allegations only have a place in a study of Hitler's career if it can be shown that [they] directly affected his political judgments and decisions'.

Whatever the reluctance stems from it seems to be time that it was overcome. It has now been shown, without much room for doubt, that he was infected. It seems equally certain that he was not treated in time to arrest the progress of the disease. Paul Ehrlich's invention of 'Salvarsan 606', which remained the standard treatment for syphilis until the arrival of Penicillin in 1943, was announced to the medical world at the Congress for Internal Medicine at Wiesbaden on 19th April 1910. But it was not generally available in mass produced form until 1912; and it is highly improbable that Hitler, even if he'd sought treatment in the earliest stages of his infection, could have afforded the necessary specialist's fees for a course of the new wonder drug. Doubtless he had every kind of treatment after he'd risen to power – the attachment to the Hitler court of venereologists as eminent as Spiethoff speaks for itself. But by then *Spirochaeta .pallida* had latched itself irremovably on to his system and nothing could have cured the damage it had caused, for the cells of the organs so attacked and destroyed are not replaced.

Thus, with evidence rather than 'allegations' set down it is reasonable to keep that evidence in mind while Hitler's political and military career is traced through its upward curve of triumph to its ignominious end in the bunker below the Chancellery on 30th April 1945, when the life of the infamous Third Reich ended as ingloriously as that of its founder after twelve years and four months instead of the thousand years he had promised,

Left and *above:* Hitler the demagogue. *Below:* The end of Hitler's Reich. The bunker in Berlin is blown up

The man

Hitler left Vienna in the spring of 1913. He had by then developed gastric troubles that doubtless were the early manifestations of his untreated syphilis. He had also concentrated within himself a great deal of the anti-Jewish feeling that prevailed in the city.

It would be stretching a point to draw the conclusion that Hitler's anti-Semitism was solely the outcome of the bitterness he felt toward Hannah the Jewish whore for infecting him. That would depend on two premises: that she had been his only sexual contact – which seems improbable; and that he was aware, then, that he'd contracted the disease – which cannot be established. There can be no doubt that by the time he was certain of his infection – had been told of it, and was being treated for it, by specialists like Spiethoff and quacks like Morell – the root of his hatred could have been fed by personal revenge; he was a spiteful man. But in 1912 it is most likely that he had merely absorbed anti-Semitism as he absorbed other ideas, having nothing original of his own to offer.

Vienna at that time was rife with it. Anti-Semitic books and pamphlets gushed from the presses – some of them pornographic, most of them insanely false in their accusations, all of them witless and insulting. Their vehemence at first astonished him: 'In the Jew I still saw only a man who was of a different religion, and therefore, on grounds of human tolerance, I was against the idea that he should be attacked because he had a different faith . . . I considered that the tone adopted by the anti-Semitic press in Vienna was unworthy of the cultural traditions of a great people.'

But it was not long before he overcame his astonishment. 'In my eyes the charge against Judaism became a grave one the moment I discovered the Jewish activities in the press, in art, in literature and the theatre.' He also discovered 'that nine tenths of all the smutty literature, artistic tripe and theatrical banalities, had to be charged to the account' of the Jews and that there was 'no form of foulness, especially in cultural life, in which at

An idealised portrait taken in 1933

20

least one Jew did not participate'.

All these remarkable discoveries, which he rants on about in the wind-blown hackneyed phrases with which *Mein Kampf* bulges, were topped by the realization 'that the Jews were the leaders of Social Democracy. In face of that revelation the scales fell from my eyes. My long inner struggle was at an end.' One can hear the scales thumping to the ground, the conflicting winds in his stomach rumbling to silence. He had at last found something to concentrate his viciousness on. But not only that. In having his mind led by way of racialism to political science he found a subject that suited both his mentality and his character. The pan-Germanic ideas that had inflected the curriculum at his Linz school now inundated his mind with swirling effect. From that vortex emerged the vision of himself as the Messianic saviour of the Aryan race – especially the German part of it. He expressed the conviction a thousand times. One of the more nauseating examples of this expression was in a pre-electoral speech in Vienna on 9th April 1938:

'I believe that it was God's will to send a boy from here into the Reich, to let him grow up, to raise him to be the leader of the nation so as to enable him to lead back his homeland into the Reich . . . to me the grace was given . . . to be able to unite my home-land with the Reich . . . may every German recognize the hour and measure its import and bow in humility before the Almighty who . . . has wrought a miracle upon us!'

That was Hitler fully developed in his megalomania. But no miracle of the Almighty had been needed to bring the embryo 'saviour' of 1912 to the megalomaniac Führer of 1938. Given a man of his instability, who was harbouring resentment against a world that failed to find any genius in him, and whose body was nurturing

Corporal Hitler (right) poses with wartime comrades

the activities of the destructive organism of syphilis, the circumstances in which such a 'saviour' could flourish had all been created by the signatories of the Treaty of Versailles.

Hitler had avoided conscription into the Austrian army in 1913 on the grounds that he refused to serve 'with filthy Czech Jews and the dregs of the Habsburg monarchy'. He left Vienna to escape service. The police, however, tenaciously pursued him with their enquiries and in January 1914 caught up with him in Munich, where he was ordered to present himself for medical examination. He was rejected, he says, because of 'poor health and general debility'. He goes on to explain that his general debility was caused by 'malnutrition consequent upon my slender earnings as an artist'. But in 1938 he ordered the Gestapo to find and destroy all records of the examination. Whatever the reason for the army's rejection of him in 1913, he was welcomed as a volunteer into the 16th Bavarian Infantry Regiment on 7th August 1914. He served as a messenger in the same regiment throughout the war, was awarded two Iron Crosses (First and Second Class) for no officially recorded reasons; and was promoted to corporal.

During a British attack on the French village of Comines on 13th October 1918 Hitler was blinded. That was the blindness mentioned in the secret report referred to by Kersten. Gas was being used by the British and it was supposed at the time to be the cause. He was sent back to hospital in Pasewalk and was there examined by an ophthalmologist, Dr Viktor Krückmann, who reported that Hitler was suffering from hysterical blindness, not from any injury caused by gas. 'It is a nervous complaint often. indicative of the tertiary stage of syphilis', he wrote. 'I advise that this man should be examined for evidence of that disease and treated accordingly. He will recover his sight.'

Which indeed he did. But of the subsequent examination by the

Venereal Diseases Clinic to which he was sent there is no record. Perhaps it too was destroyed by the Gestapo. It may have been seen by the compiler of the secret document examined by Kersten, for Kersten refers to its mention of 'symptoms associated with syphilis'. But Krückmann gave it as his opinion, in 1965, that it was deliberately destroyed, just as the records of Spiethoff's consultations were destroyed, by Frick.

At all events, Hitler was still in the Pasewalk hospital when the armistice was proclaimed, peace having been sought by General Ludendorff of the German High Command and the Chancellor, Prince Max of Baden.

Above left: Hitler (back row, extreme right) convalescing after being wounded, 1916. *Below left:* Ludendorff attacks in March 1918. *Below:* By August 1918, the Allies have counter-attacked; German resistance begins to crumble. German prisoners taken during August 1918

'In November', Hitler wrote, 'the general tension increased. Then one day disaster broke in upon us without warning. Sailors came in motor lorries and called on us to rise in revolt. A few Jew-boys were the leaders . . . Not one of them had seen active service at the front. Through the medium of a hospital for venereal diseases these three Orientals had been sent back home. Now their red flags were being hoisted here.'

There is no evidence whatever, other than Hitler's spitting contempt, that any Jews were involved, that they were non-combatants and 'orientals', or that they had been at a hospital for venereal diseases. (Had he perhaps seen them there?) The revolutionary sailors were merely a splinter group of the mutineers at Kiel who had refused to take out their ships to continue a battle that was over. But that is just an example of Hitler's maniacal prejudices.

In a great slab of ill-chosen words he goes on to say that he was recover-

ing his sight and that he could scarcely believe that Germany had capitulated. 'I staggered and stumbled back to my ward and buried my aching head between the blankets and pillow . . . So all had been in vain. In vain all the sacrifices and privations, in vain the hunger and thirst for endless months, in vain those hours that we stuck to our posts though the fear of death gripped our souls . . .', and so on in an elongated saga of self-pity disguised as vengeful breast-beating. Apart from its sidelight on the character of its author that chapter of *Mein Kampf* has only one significant phrase: 'For my part I then decided that I would take up political work'.

The capitulation that so shocked Hitler – and indeed the whole German nation, which had supposed that German victory was in sight – was instigated as early as 5th October 1918. On that date a note was despatched to President Woodrow Wilson of the United States formally asking for peace negotiations. Wilson replied asking whether the German govern-

ment intended discussing peace on the terms of his addresses to Congress in which were stated the famous Fourteen Points, Four Principles and Five Particulars. The answer was Yes. Thus it was initially agreed between Germany and the United States that the peace negotiations should be based on a total of twenty-three conditions laid down by Wilson which would have to be accepted by the Allies also. It was a shaky foundation for the discussion of a Treaty of Peace – particularly as the Allies had had nothing but the slenderest indication that the United States had a basis of negotiation with the enemy. Nor, when they heard the conditions,

Below: The victors dictate peace.
Lloyd George, Orlando, Clemenceau, Wilson at Versailles, 1919
Above Right: The German delegation at Versailles. Hitler called them 'the November criminals';
Below Right : Germany's air force reduced to kindling

were they by any means inclined to accept them. Every one of the Fourteen Points was turned inside out, upside down and sideways by Clemenceau of France, Lloyd George of Britain, and Sonnino of Italy, each of whom had reasons – not all of them admirable reasons – for wishing to amend the Fourteen Points to gain specific advantages for their individual nations. But America remained adamant. The Fourteen Points must be accepted *in toto* or a separate peace would be concluded with Germany.

'This was a bombshell', says Richard M Watt in *The Kings Depart*. 'Lloyd George and Clemenceau could not possibly allow themselves to be put into the position of refusing a victorious armistice and compelling their nations to continue a now pointless war – especially when their reasons for doing so would be interpreted by world opinion as a cynical rejection of such exalted principles as freedom of the seas and the abolition of secret diplomacy. [They had been] placed in a position from which there was no escape'.

It was now the turn of the Allies to capitulate. They accepted the Wilson principles and the armistice was concluded on 11th November. It was the opening of the door to the Versailles peace conference.

About that disastrous conference and the Treaty that was signed at it, after five months of wrangling, volumes have been written. It is necessary to say in summary only that of the conditions laid down by Wilson and accepted by the Germans no more than four were ultimately incorporated in the Treaty. The defeated enemy had signed an armistice on terms that were twisted beyond all recognition by the time the Treaty was signed. During the five months of wrangling there had been revealed attitudes of bitterness, greed and gloating revenge that, though in a way understandable, could have led only to

The Nazi leader in Bavarian *Lederhosen*

contention in the future – however long the clash could be postponed.

Of the plenipotentiaries of the thirty-two nations assembled at the conference Lord Keynes wrote: 'The future life of Europe was not their concern; its means of livelihood was not their anxiety. Their preoccupations, good and bad alike, related to frontiers and nationalities, to the balance of power, to imperial aggrandisements, to the future enfeeblement of a strong and dangerous enemy, to revenge, and to the shifting by the victors of their unbearable financial burdens on to the shoulders of the defeated.'

And as a further indictment of the Treaty the Prime Minister of Italy, Signor Nitti, later wrote: 'It will remain for ever a terrible precedent in modern history that, against all pledges, all precedents and traditions, the representatives of Germany were never even heard; nothing was left to them but to sign a treaty at a moment when famine and exhaustion and threat of revolution made it impossible not to sign it . . . In the old law of the Church it was laid down that everyone must have a hearing, even the devil. But the new democracy, which proposed to install the League of Nations, did not even obey the precepts which the dark Middle Ages held sacred on behalf of the accused.'

It was upon the scene created from the shambles of violated agreements, tyrannical statesmen, pistol-point force, and the dangerous humiliation of a vanquished nation, that Hitler, the man of destiny, appeared to 'take up political work'.

Hitler's greatest asset – and it amounted in its field to genius – was his psychological insight. Seeing himself as a man rejected by society, and blindly ignoring the fact that that rejection was caused by his own unendearing nature, he was readily able to identify himself with the masses of a nation that, merely seeking an honourable peace, had been kicked and ground into the dust by the

Versailles Treaty. Humiliation is the most dangerous of all punishments to mete out to a nation not abject in character; and a man who can play on the emotions of a people forced to grovel cannot fail to find a hearing. Certainly not in the circumstances afflicting post-war Germany.

But it was by no means an immediate hearing. Even an inherent genius has to be guided along a profitable path. So far as Hitler was concerned the path lay through the taverns of Munich where, in 1919, he fortuitously found himself among men who later were to become famous as his teachers and associates – Dietrich Eckart, Ernst Röhm, Alfred Rosenberg, Rudolf Hess, Anton Drexler, Karl Harer, and Gottfried Feder. Those men – a poet, a soldier, an architect, a politician disguised as a military adviser, a locksmith, a journalist, and a slightly dotty scientist-cum-economist – were all floundering in a treacly mess of misbegotten revolutionary notions for the rescue of Germany from the disastrous state of affairs wrought by the war and the Treaty of Peace.

It was Eckart who fidgeted endlessly over the formation of a 'German Citizen Party' to counteract the influence of Bolsheviks and Jews, and who described the character of the man who must lead it:

'We must have a fellow at the top who won't wince at the rattle of a machine-gun. The mob must be given a damned good fright. An officer won't do; the people don't respect them any more. Best of all would be a workman in a soldier's coat and with his tongue in his cheek. He needn't be very brainy; politics is the most imbecile business in the world and every market-woman in Munich knows as much as those fellows in Weimar. I'd rather have a stupid, vain jackanapes who can give the Reds a juicy

'We must have a fellow at the top who won't wince at the rattle of a machine gun'

answer and not run away whenever a chair-leg is aimed at him, than a dozen learned professors who sit trembling on the wet trousers-seat of facts. Also he must be a bachelor. Then we shall get the women!'

But it was Anton Drexler who actually founded the party that Hitler was to lead, the German Workers' Party, a lacklustre, static group with forty members and a total capital of 7.50 marks. And it was while attending one of its feeble political meetings on 12th September 1919 that he spoke with such vehemence that Drexler persuaded him to join the committee of six. He had been sent to the meeting as a minor spy in the service of the Munich army command, which was prodding to detect subversive political activities. But what he actually detected was the chance of a lifetime. Here was an aimless, poorly conducted organization full of nonentities; and although he was himself a nonentity he had ideas far above that station and immediately saw the possibility of imposing them on a floundering body that lacked leadership, energy and members.

Almost at once he assumed command; implicitly if not by title; and three months later he was appointed Propaganda Officer. (Hitler's brilliance as publicist has been fully explored in *The Nuremberg Rallies*, Campaign Book 8 in this series.) He brought about the amalgamation with several other minor movements whose aims, vaguely, were the practical implementation of a policy of anti-Semitism and anti-Communism, and the non-fulfilment of the oppressive conditions of the Versailles Treaty. And he blew up the title into the grandiose *Nationalsozialistische Deutsche Arbeiterpartei*, (National Socialist German Workers' Party), from the first word of which the abbreviation Nazi was manufactured. The fortunes of the Nazi Party, and subsequently of the Third Reich, over the next twenty-five years, are the fortunes of Adolf Hitler.

The demagogue

Like Hitler, the Party was diseased. It was the disease of neurotic vainglory. Those with an interest in the study of theories of racialism can examine the symptoms exhibited by such mighty bores as Thomas Wolfe, Houston Stewart Chamberlain, the Comte de Gobineau and Chamberlain's father-in-law Richard Wagner. They all lead back to the myths of heroic Aryan Siegfrieds, hideous racially inferior Alberichs, and Valhallas fit for triumphant German gods to live in. People dissatisfied with reality create legends; and the wretched realities of the Versailles Treaty and the Weimar Republic impelled every kind of sick grievance needing only the solace of a taletelling healer to ease the malaise. Houston Stewart Chamberlain, after having his boots unctuously glossed with Hitler's lick-spittle admiration, declared:

'The fact that at the hour of her deepest need Germany has given birth to a Hitler proves her vitality.'

What it in fact proved was the Party's inability to provide any alternative to the vindictive evils into which Germany had been ground by Versailles other than the falsely glamorous Valhalla now revealed in prestigious glimpses by the marketing methods of their Pied Piper saviour.

In the same way in which Hitler had assumed command of the nonentities of the German Workers' Party in 1919, he had by 1923 gathered in his wake some 55,000 unorganized Germans – most of them from the south – who, characteristically malleable, were easily shaped to the aggressive Nazi pattern. His first attempt at overt aggression was to surround himself with a body of witless roughnecks and burst into a Munich hall where a political meeting was being staged by a rival group. He fired pistol shots at the ceiling, shrieked out that the Bavarian government was now deposed, and that he himself was the leader of the new Reich. Understandably, this melodramatic coup failed (though only just), and to save face he staged a demonstration march next day, 9th November 1923. That march, which he led side by side with Ludendorff, encountered thin police resistance and shots were fired from both sides. Hitler bolted, leaving the bodies of sixteen dead Nazis in the Odeonplatz. (They were later to be made the most famous martyrs of the Nazi cause, and Hitler was to justify his unseemly disappearance from the fray by explaining that he had 'carried a helpless child out of the firing line'. There was no child; and if there had been, Hitler could not have carried it because before bolting he had fallen heavily and dislocated his right shoulder and broken his left arm.)

The direct result of the 9th Novem-

Houston Stewart Chamberlain

Richard Wagner

ber *putsch* was that Hitler was arrested for treason, tried and given a mandatory sentence of five years' imprisonment, and confined in the greatest comfort in Landsberg fortress. He was allowed special food, visitors, a comfortable room, flowers, a private secretary, and unlimited exercise in the grounds; and was released after eight months, his defence speech to the Munich People's Court having been so full of lofty patriotic guff that their verdict of 'guilty' had been found only after assurances from the president that the accused would be granted an early pardon.

During his imprisonment he wrote – if it can be called writing – the tedious *Mein Kampf*. The Party had been proscribed, but its surreptitious revival had been the matter of much quarrelling among some of Hitler's leading henchmen – Strasser, Streicher, Röhm, Rosenberg, Ludendorff, Feder and Frick – who fought over the political corpse like hyenas. Hitler loftily dissociated himself from their disagreements on aims and leadership and engaged in the literary life, dictating much of *Mein Kampf* to Rudolf Hess, who acted as his secretary. It was no wish of his to have the Party come to life again under someone else's leadership. He waited till he was released on parole then persuaded the Bavarian Minister

of Justice to allow the re-formation of the Party and the re-publication of its newspaper the *Volkischer Beobachter*. His persuasion was based on an admission of all his past mistakes and a declaration that the Nazis had only the single object of fighting Marxism and Judaism. There was a glutinous reconciliation between him and some of the bickering leaders, and the Party was once again a force in the field.

For a long time, though, it was an extremely ineffective force. Though he had acceded to Hitler's abject pleas, the Minister of Justice had not been so stupid as to allow him to make speeches. That was very wise. It was only the mesmeric personality projected through the hysterical speeches that brought the Party its adherents. But wisdom could not be sustained. The ban on Hitler's speeches was lifted in May 1927 and the quasi-religious cult of the saviour spread among thousands more who listened to him with an hysteria matching his own – an hysteria which was, as Hitler himself put it, not involuntary but 'a tactic based on the precise calculation of all human weaknesses, the results of which must lead almost mathematically to success'.

Which of course it did. He was a rapist using a phallus of words. Eckhart had been fortuitously right when he had drawn the pattern for the leader: 'He must be a bachelor. Then we shall get the women!' The masses were indeed to him 'women'. Coarse jokes were made about his own statement that after a big speech he was 'soaking wet'; but it was true that he experienced orgiastic delirium – 'a substitute', as Joachim Fest has put it, 'for the emotional experience that had remained closed to him in all his monstrous egofixation'. Possibly, too, if one concedes that he was a rapist, also an act of revenge against the syphilitic Hannah. He had written feverishly in *Mein Kampf* on syphilis and Jewish genetics, and that too may have been subconscious - or even deliberate – vengeance on a person rather than a race.

As for more normal sexual relationships, there has been much speculation about Hitler's explorations in that direction, but very few known facts to support it. In his youth there was the unattainable Stefanie and the all-too-easily attainable Hannah; in middle age his supposed mistress Eva Braun, whom he married as a prelude to the suicide pact that ended their lives. And during the days of the rise of the Party in the late 1920s he lived with his niece, Geli Raubal, daughter of his step-sister Angela. Geli shot herself in Hitler's flat in Munich in 1931 and for a time he appeared to be inconsolable; but that proves nothing except an emotional fixation on a girl twenty years younger than himself whom he had characteristically tyrannized into a state of neurotic subjection. Because of its deteriorative effect on his mind and body, the brief encounter with Hannah is enormously important; but all other sidelights on Hitler's sexual endeavours can be switched to the realm of conjecture.

In contrast, everything about the mesmeric influence and growth of the Party under Hitler's leadership .is supported by facts. There were minor disagreements within the organization – mainly centred in the raffish Storm Troopers who had been recruited from the ex-service men who formed the tiny army permitted by the Versailles Treaty and who displayed more military than political enthusiasm, which at the time didn't suit Hitler's book at all. (Hitler allowed them to choke themselves with their own war-cries and by 1929 had set up his own *corps d'élite* under the sinister leadership of Heinrich Himmler. The SS – *Schutz Staffeln* or blackshirted bodyguard – had political enthusiasm enough and were sworn to absolute obedience; and it was eventually through them that Hitler dominated Party, nation and armed forces.) In spite of such internal discord, however, the Party increased its grip on the country. Having fallen to 17,000 in 1926, the restoration in 1927 of Hitler's right to make public speeches quickly brought the membership to 60,000 in 1928; and one may certainly infer at least twice that number who were supporters if not actual members of the Party.

But it was with the American financial crisis of 1929, and the succeeding economic depression in the West, that Hitler and the Nazi Party rose to victory. Under the Weimar Republic, which Hitler referred to variously as the 'republic of betrayal', 'the November criminals' and 'the Jew-ridden traitors', American money had poured into Germany. The mark had been stabilized; Allied forces withdrawn from the Rhineland, and industrial production increased to an extent that had reduced unemployment to little more than half a million. Against such prosperity the Nazis had little hope of making much headway with their doom-laden prophecies of forthcoming financial disaster. They polled fewer than a million votes at the 1928 elections and were represented by only twelve seats in the Reichstag. But with the Wall Street crash of 1929 disaster came. Germany's inability to repay either the iniquitous reparations demanded by the Versailles Treaty or the interest on the short-term loans that

Above: Hitler, Julius Streicher, and other leaders at a German Day rally, September, 1923. *Below:* The treason trial following the unsuccessful Munich putsch of November 1923, Ludendorff arrives at the court

Above: With party comrades during his imprisonment at Landsberg (Hess second from right). *Below:* In 1927, after having spoken in Berlin for the first time

Eva Braun with Hitler

eli Raubal, Hitler's niece and greatest love.

Left: Now Reich Chancellor, Hitler greets the ageing President Hindenburg, 1933 *Above:* Rapturous crowds greet their Führer

had so readily been made by an America dizzy with her own power, ensured an immediate economic plunge. She was like a man who has been leapfrogging cheques into and out of his bank account and is suddenly let down by the non-arrival of the credit intended to cover the post-dated debit made the day before yesterday and due to be presented today. By 1932 there were five million unemployed. The disease of hopelessness spread throughout the country. Food, warmth and shelter were pulled out of the people's grasp with terrible frequency. Even if a breadwinner was working he was unlikely to be working on full time. Savings vanished in a wave of profiteering and a desperate effort to pay the mortgages on farms and houses. And, as Alan Bullock says in *Hitler: a Study in Tyranny:*

'Like men and women in a town stricken by an earthquake, millions of Germans saw the apparently solid framework of their existence cracking and crumbling. In such circumstances men are no longer amenable to the arguments of reason. In such circumstances men entertain fantastic fears, extravagant hatreds and extravagant hopes. In such circumstances the extravagant demagogy of Hitler began to attract a mass following as it had never done before.'

That mass following, coupled with the inability of his opponents to compete with his propaganda methods, and reinforced by his own cunning intrigues to subvert – by threat, bribery, murder or any other method that served the purpose – the efforts of those Party members who were themselves jostling for power, brought Hitler to the Chancellorship of the German Reich in January 1933. On the death of President von Hindenberg nineteen months later he announced – with the coerced agreement of those who had in some ways attempted to restrain his rise to power – that the offices of President and Chancellor were united and that he himself was now Supreme ruler of the State and Commander-in-Chief of all the armed forces.

His first command to his army was to swear an oath of allegiance and obedience to him personally – not to

Below: Hitler's first cabinet. Göring and Papen in front row. *Above:* 13th June 1934, Hitler warns the Reichstag that 'the Wehrmacht is the only instrument of war.'*Right:*On 30th June, Ernst Röhm (right) and many of his SA lieutenants are summarily executed

the Constitution or the country:

'I swear by God this holy oath: I will render unconditional obedience to the Führer of the German Reich and People, Adolf Hitler, the Supreme Commander of the Armed Forces, and will be ready, as a brave soldier, to give my life at any time for my Führer.'

Thus, by August 1934, Adolf Hitler had manoeuvred himself into a position of absolute power. The corruptive effects of that power were soon to become apparent.

Hitler's personal ruthlessness toward rivals or dissentients had been shockingly manifested in a purge five weeks earlier. On 30th June he ordered the execution of Ernst Röhm and other leaders of the Storm Troopers who had attempted a revolt. There were massacres all over Germany. The ex-Chancellor, General von Schleicher, and prominent army officers, civil servants and Roman Catholics were murdered. The assassins were the black-shirted SS who, together with the Gestapo, were from now on to become the chief executants of Hitler's machinations.

Politically and socially there were less murderous but equally effective forms of ruthlessness. The entire parliamentary system of the Weimar republic was dissolved. All political parties except the Nazis were banned. To found any kind of non-Nazi political organization became punishable by heavy terms of imprisonment. Freedom of cultural expression in art and literature was no more. Civil rights and equality of citizenship were suppressed and the 'leader' system introduced – an all-powerful Führer at the top and innumerable lesser Führers step-dancing on the heads of their inferiors in rank right down to the ordinary citizen for whom there could be no leadership until he had found someone to lead. Institutions such as education, Church and press were revolutionized. Only the Nazi version of Germany's history was

Indem ich mich des Juden erwehre kämpfe ich für das Werk des Herrn

Anti-Semitic propaganda. *Left:* 'By resisting the Jews I fight for the Lord' proclaims a banner. *Above:* Der Stürmer displayed on a Berlin notice-board

told, only the anti-Jewish religion of propaganda was tolerated, the press was the mouthpiece of Nazidom and no other voice was to be heard.

For four years Hitler built up the Nazi state into a diplomatic and military machine that violated most of the principal clauses of the Versailles Treaty. He founded the Luftwaffe, introduced military conscription, occupied the demilitarized Rhineland with his troops; he withdrew from the world disarmament conference, abandoned Germany's membership of the League of Nations, concluded a prestigious concordat with the Vatican and a non-aggression pact with Poland – both of which were meant to allow time for his designs to mature, not to give Italy or Poland any peaceful advantages.

Those four years from 1933 to 1937 saw the economic recovery of the German nation and the swelling of her armed forces to an immense aggressive power that baffled and frustrated the member countries of the League of Nations (from which Japan and Italy, as well as Germany, had resigned). Hitler's psychological insight had proved to be brilliant. With a series of bold strokes of diplomacy he had foxed the statesmen who played the diplomatic game by conventional rules. By the time they had shaken off their gentlemenly attitude and realized that they were dealing with a brilliant psychopath the strands of the Führer's plans for German domination had become inextricably knotted round the unwary victims. By the spring of 1938 Hitler was strong enough to bring off a bloodless invasion of Austria and annex it into the German Reich. Henceforward the land of his own birth ceased to exist as a name.

But his maniacal lust for *lebensraum* and power were by no means so

45

German rearmament. *Above:* Hitler reviews new Wehrmacht units. *Below:* Infantry and PzKpfw III tanks give a battle demonstration. Nuremberg 1938

German conquest. *Above:* The Anschluss of Austria, March 1938. *Below:* Hitler rides in triumph through Carlsbad, Czechoslovakia, October 1938

easily sated. Britain and France
having pusillanimously betrayed
Czechoslovakia into withdrawing her
defensive forces from the Sudetenland
to give themselves time to prepare for
a war whose inevitability they had
ensured, Hitler occupied that territory without having to strike a blow,
in the autumn of 1938. Six months
later he spread his talons into
Bohemia, Moravia and Memel. The
Free State of Danzig was proclaimed
part of the German Reich on 1st
September 1939, and Poland was invaded without warning or provocation
at dawn on the same day, thus forcing
Britain and France to declare war to
back their treaty obligations to Poland.

A week before the holocaust of war
was loosed upon Europe Hitler had
brought off his crowning stroke of diplomacy: a non-aggression and trade
pact with Russia 'guaranteeing' peace
between the two countries for a mini-
mum of ten years. Since he had been
preaching against the wickedness of
Communism since 1919 the pact was a
masterstroke. The theoretical cost of
it was considerable: nothing less than
the division of the ill-fated Poland into
two equal parts – the easternmost of
which would be Russia's prize. But the
worthlessness of the Pact can be
measured by Hitler's revelation of his
eventual aim, made at a conference
with his military chiefs on 22nd
August: 'My pact is only meant to
stall for time, gentlemen. We will
crush the Soviet Union'. Time indeed
was of the essence for his schemes.
For Germany to fight, even in her
present state of immense military
power, on both Western and Eastern
fronts simultaneously would have
been as fatal in 1939 as it had proved to
be in the First World War. The West
must be crushed first. And immediately he received the Allies'
declaration of war on 3rd September
1939 Hitler set about his gigantic task.

The General

With his attack upon Poland Hitler had not only precipitated the war but could claim that no state of war had existed until the Allies declared it. Reduced to the status of a children's backyard fight, it was '*I* didn't start it, *he* did'. The invasion of Poland was merely, by Hitlerian standards, a logical and justifiable extension of his claim to the Free State of Danzig and, earlier, to Austria, the Sudetenland, Bohemia, Moravia and Memel. These, as he had argued interminably, were part of the German Reich, from which they had been chipped away in the rapacious carve-up after the First World War. He could also point to the fact that not a drop of blood had been shed in his 'liberation' of their people from the oppressive yoke of Versailles. Had the Poles shown a similar sensible willingness to be embraced by the Reich there would have been no need for coercion.

The speciousness of such argument would of course have been apparent to any impartial tribunal investigating the immediate causes of the war. But there was no such tribunal and no such argument.

Poland was virtually conquered within a matter of hours. Mastery of the air was easily attained by an all-out offensive beginning at dawn on 1st September. Waves of bombers simply flew over Polish aerodromes and bombed the planes on the ground. Those that got into the air were shot down by the bombers' fighter escorts, which then descended to roof-top level and machine-gunned the planes and personnel that had survived the bombing. With no defence against further air attacks the Poles then were completely vulnerable so far as bridges, marshalling yards, production centres, military installations and mobile columns were concerned. The Polish defence forces numbered nearly two million; but the German air attack had ensured that they could not be effectively mobilized, since all communications were thrown into utter confusion.

No aspect of the Polish campaign should have surprised anybody, least

The corporal and his generals. Hitler with Blomberg and Fritsch before their dismissal

Spearhead of the blitzkrieg. *Above:* Me-109E fighters and Me-110 fighter bombers over Poland. *Right:* Stukas approach their target

of all the Poles. It was entirely consistent with Hitler's methods. (The Russians, despite being bonded with Germany by the non-aggression pact, were, in less than two years' time, to experience precisely the same way of opening the attack upon them by the bombing of their aerodromes; and they were equally unprepared.) But the Polish forces were being assembled to defend a leisurely attack by the traditional methods of 1914. Their Commander-in-Chief, Marshal Smigly-Rydz, seems first to have been disarmed – in the non-military sense – by Hitler's assurance given via Göring in 1937 that Germany had no territorial interest in Poland, and secondly, when attack by Germany was clearly imminent, to have supposed that the attack would go by the rules of the 1914 book.

It may seem somewhat feeble to point through the glass of hindsight to Hitler's obvious contempt for the rules of any outmoded book that did not, so to speak, suit his own book. But clearly it was not obvious, or else was incredible, at the time. Not only the Polish but the military theorists of Britain and France too suffered from the hangover of thinking in terms of cavalry charges and other outmoded ploys; and in the early stages of the war were continually dumbfounded by Hitler's ruthless but perfectly logical planning and execution.

That skill has since come to be marvelled at as Hitler's 'intuition'. There has been a tendency to suppose that he had some almost supernatural power that enabled him to anticipate the military moves of his opponents – or, rather, in the early stages of the war, the lack of any ability on the part of his mightiest opponents, the French, to make any moves at all except of the most pusillanimous kind. But Hitler had no supernatural powers. He was not in league with any necromancers. His 'intuition' was no more than the psychological insight that had enabled him to identify himself with the nation humiliatingly vanquished by Versailles. It was simply a sound understanding of human nature in general and of his opponents' characters in particular. (It was not, in the particular sense, an unfailing understanding, as was to be proved by his ignorance of the American character; but its occasional failures proved that there was nothing supernatural about it.) Just as he knew, and had unequivocally stated in *Mein Kampf*, that the endless reiteration of a demonstrable lie turns it effectively into a demonstrable truth, so he knew that he had virtually nothing to fear from the French in 1939.

He had correctly deduced that after the First World War the French would be obsessed with defence, with security within their own boundaries. The two successive post-war Commanders-in-Chief, Pétain and Weygand, had made it very clear. The people had seen the futile massacre of French youth in the bloody offensive designed by General Nivelle in 1917; they were in no heart to tolerate any more Generals of like mind. Nor had they any interest in extending their frontiers. They would spend years licking their terrible wounds and millions of francs barricading themselves in. The French Third Republic was in danger of collapse and the dignity of French civilization had been cracked by a profitless victory in 1918. Only mighty bastions behind which they could brood and build up a huge army of defending Frenchmen would satisfy the nation.

In all this Hitler was correct – and indeed it needed little in the way of psychological understanding to perceive the obvious. The impregnable fortifications to be built in the name

Germany, Aug.1939

Apr. 1940   Dates of German Occupation
or Invasion

0 Miles   100   200   300   400
0 Kilometres 200   400   600

Kristiansand   Trondhei
Andalsne

NORWA
Bergen   Apr. 1940
Oslo

Stavanger

NORTH SEA

DENMAR
Apr. 1940

EIRE
Dublin

GREAT

BRITAIN

London

Amsterdam   May 1940

Hamburg

Mar. 1936
RHINELAND   GERM

NETH.

Calais   BELG.
Dieppe   Brussels   Cologne   Weimar

Cherbourg

Brest   BRITTANY   Le Havre   LUX.   Wiesbaden
Caen   Soissons   Frankfurt
NORMANDY   Compiegne   SIEGFRIED   Nuremburg
Paris   LINE
Seine   Karlsruhe

Meuse

MAGINOT
LINE   Braun

Nantes   Landsberg   Munich
Berchtesgade

FRANCE   Berne   AU
SWITZ.

May 1940

Milan

ATLANTIC

OCEAN

Lisbon   Madrid   Corsica
Rom

PORTUGAL   SPAIN

Sardinia

Gibraltar

MEDITERRANEAN SEA

ALGERIA

Above: Smigly-Rydz, the Polish commander *Left:* Panzer troops rest on their advance into Poland

of the War Minister, André Maginot, were begun in 1930.

Superficially, the Maginot Line made up in impregnability for what it lacked in sense. (It left undefended the frontier to Belgium, through whose militarily ideal terrain the Germans had since time immemorial always attacked France.) But impregnability in this case was nothing but a comforting illusion, an almost literal sticking of heads into the sand – for the elaborate fortifications were built deep into the ground. They were burrows fitted out with stores and ammunition, with comforts and communications to withstand any siege. The mighty guns of the Line faced Germany and were protected by impenetrable steel and concrete. The 'tombstone of France' – as Major-General J F C Fuller has called it – had cost some £40,000,000, which is a lot of money for a soporific; but that is what it turned out to be. The French did not want to fight; their enormous army – there were at least twenty-six Divisions in the Maginot Line alone – was

Left: Weygand (second from right) with Briand, Lloyd George, and Foch. *Above:* Pétain

Above: André Maginot, French Minister of War in the early thirties. *Left:* A section of the Maginot line

riddled with treachery from top to bottom and wanted nothing more active (as Fuller put it) than to 'sit in the Maginot Line, snip up *La Vie Parisienne,* decorate their dugouts with very unsatisfying young ladies, and cry to go home'.

By the time the Maginot Line was finished in 1935 Hitler was in complete power as Führer, Chancellor, President, absolute despot and Pied Piper of the German nation. This unlovable man had succeeded, like a carrier of typhoid, in spreading the disease of vainglory among the Party, and with the help of skilful publicists like Göbbels and monstrous jamborees like the Nuremberg Rallies, would spread it throughout the nation – aided by the national susceptibility to wallow in the myth of the Master Race. In doing that he had forged a mighty sword. It was the sword of confidence. Mesmerised by their Führer's ceaseless reiteration of the theme and the endless chain of variations upon it the Germans danced to the tune of ecstatic triumph.

The confidence of France being reposed in nothing but the impregnability of the Maginot Line, it is not surprising to hear Hitler saying to the British journalist G Ward Price at Berchtesgaden in 1938, 'I have studied the Maginot Line and learned much from it'. The much he had learned from it came from very little study. The Line ended where the Belgian frontier began; there was no need to study it any more. As for the vast numbers of French soldiers locked defensively in it, 'It is an axiom of the art of war that the side which stays within its fortifications is beaten'. The tag was Napoleon's but the truth of it was as old as war. Only a minuscule number of French militarists unburied their heads from the Maginot sands long enough to shout words of warning. One was Colonel de Gaulle, another was General Guillaumat:'It is dangerous to let the false and demoralizing notion spread that once we have fortifications the inviola-

59

The SS became the Nazi élite. *Above:* Hitler's personal SS bodyguard. *Below* and *right:* Himmler grew to be one of the most powerful men in the Nazi hierarchy

bility of our country is assured, and that they are a substitute for the rude labour of preparation of wills, hearts and minds'. No-one heeded the shouts. The French people were asleep, drugged by their Maginot potion. They were morally rotten, physically flabby, and apparently mentally deficient.

It is the business of a general, as the historian Polybius pointed out two thousand years ago, to create a warlike spirit, 'for of all the forces in war that is the most influential'. It is also the business of the general to turn to his own advantage those weapons aligned against him. For the first, Hitler had built up the morale of the German people to a state that was equivalent to numerical superiority in men and weapons; for the second, *inter alia* he had intrigued to infiltrate the hostile ideology of Communism into France, where it had completed the demoralization of the people with its taint. Thus, up to 3rd Spetember 1939, he had created favourable conditions. But with the invasion of Poland and the inevitable consequent declaration of war by France and Britain he had forced an issue that would put his generalship to a greater test.

It was one of Hitler's characteristics that he could not delegate. It was a natural corollary of his despotism. He wanted to make all the decisions and take all the responsibility; and if he had been able to assume god-like control of everything from the grand strategy to the design of his troops' buttons he would have been a god-like general. Intervening between him and that state, however, were the generals of his High Command, who were merely human, with no god-like aspirations, and who were much abler administrators than their Führer, who hated systematic work as much as he hated delegation of power.

Normal military practice is to appoint commanders for their expertise

When giving speeches or holding conferences, Hitler often worked himself up into a state of frenzy

in various aspects of strategic affairs, to consult them, and to co-ordinate their advice. An overall plan of campaign is then evolved and the commanders directed to carry it out in its various stages.

Hitler worked the other way round. His hatred of delegation was based on distrust. Like all megalomaniacs he was fearful of rivalry, of any other hand than his own on the reins of power. When in Landsberg fortress he had cunningly detached himself from all attempts by his henchmen to revive the proscribed Nazi party because he could not himself have led it while still serving a prison sentence. After his release, though, he set about the restoration of the Party, and his own leadership of it, very swiftly. And his achievement of absolute political power during the first half of the nineteen-thirties was crowned by his own decree, which stated unquivocally: 'From henceforth I exercise personally the immediate command over the whole armed forces'.

Since even Hitler could see the impracticability of extending his command like a web throughout all the ramifications of organization, he made a gesture to military orthodoxy by establishing a High Command. It was, however, a body controlled by Hitler's lackey favourites rather than a consultative and advisory committee rich with influence. It served as a computer to work out the details of Hitler's grand designs. It also reported to him what was practical and what not, and in that sense may perhaps be said to have been advisory. But its master's mind was already made up on every point. When decision coincided with advice the High Command appeared to be working in the orthodox way; when its recommendations were torn to shreds in turbulent scenes at what with Hitler passed for 'conferences', and he spat out his refusal to consider any question of emendation – then the Führer appeared to be ironwilled and brilliantly perceptive in a setup that surrounded him with blockheads.

Naturally the army chiefs were often aroused to bitter resentment by such treatment. They were, after all, experienced strategists who could present an appreciation of any military situation. To be contemptuously treated because their appreciations took no account of the political manoeuvres of statesmen was humiliating. And humiliation, as had been proved by the entire course of post-Versailles German history, is extremely dangerous. It resulted in brooding conspiracies that were eventually suppressed only by the infiltration of Himmler's secret police into the armed forces. Some were never entirely suppressed in spite of the SS chief's serpentine activities. A plot to kidnap and overthrow Hitler was – ironically – frustrated only by Chamberlain's trembling supplications at Munich in 1938. The attempted murder in the bomb plot of 20th July 1944 failed only in the degree

of its effectiveness. And there were at least five other attempts on his life.

All dictators are subject to the envious attempts of rival megalomaniacs to usurp their power; but those of Hitler's generals who plotted against him were more concerned to abort the disasters they saw germinate in his decisions. They insistently advised him against attacking Czechoslovakia in 1938. 'He was like a man demented', says Brauchitsch, Commander-in-Chief of the army, of an occasion when the High Command was standing firm. 'He was sweating and shrieking, there was froth on his lips, his speech was incoherent for many minutes. Only after a frightening storm did we make out that it was "his unalterable will to smash Czechoslovakia by military action in the near future".'

The frustrating thing for the High Command was that Hitler was proved right time and time again. It was only because he had weakened their

Left: The newly re-armed Wehrmacht enters the Rhineland. *Above:* The SA, at first the Army's main threat

tactical brilliance by his distrust that their function as a consultative and administrative body failed him when most needed in the later vital campaigns of the war. But none of them could deny that, rightly or wrongly, 'He carried on his own back' (as Alan Clark says in *Barbarossa*) 'the responsibility for every decision of importance and formulated in his own mind the development of his strategic ambition in its entirety'.

His contempt for the High Command was often voiced in such inaccurate generalisations as: 'No general will ever pronounce himself ready to attack; and no commander will ever fight a defensive battle without looking over his shoulder to a "shorter line".' He was himself an inspired amateur of military strategy. He knew all the theories according to

Clausewitz, the classic battles of Darius and Alexander, the manoeuvres of Hannibal at Cannae and Frederick the Great at Leuthen; and though he very rarely visited the front line throughout the war he had a sound understanding of the fighting soldier and his needs. He had, after all, been one himself; and presumably his Iron Cross had been awarded for some act of courage, though the citation was never publicized. (Perhaps it was suppressed as unworthy by the burrowing Gestapo men who in 1938 had destroyed the records of his 1914 medical examination and the records of the Venereal Diseases Clinic to which he was sent in 1918.) Anyway, one may look charitably upon his somewhat speedy departure from the scene of action on 9th November 1923 and say that courage is a virtue only insofar as it is directed by prudence.

The ways in which he expressed his contempt for the High Command are less revealing than the reasons for it.

65

One must include among possible reasons the adolescent hatred he had felt for the officer class exemplified by the corseted, scented socialites who had, he believed, stolen Stefanie's affections. Also, there was plenty of evidence that in the First World War the German General Staff had hastened America's entry into the war by introducing unrestricted submarine attacks; had destroyed hopes of peace with Russia by demanding that a Kingdom of Poland should be established and by returning Lenin and his émigré colleagues from Geneva to Russia in 1917; and had mis-managed the Verdun battle of 1916 and thus prolonged the war. Those were errors of political and military strategy that justified censoriousness. But there was a deeper-rooted cause of his contempt: the reactionary spirit that, he said, riddled the upper echelons of the army as a result of 'Habsburg effeteness, Jewish cunning, and the Masonic disease of favouritism in high places'.

Whether his contempt was at bottom much more than a manifestation of his megalomania can be left for the moment. On the Allies' declaration of war on 3rd September 1939 Hitler could well afford to laugh in his Generals' faces. They had no record of brilliance to justify themselves. Such appreciations as they had put before him during the founding of their Führer's 'Thousand-year Reich' had been discarded with despotic fury or coldly ignored. From the time when they had advised against the reoccupation of the Rhineland as the first extension of Reich tentacles, to their recent insistent warnings against attacking Czechoslovakia they had been wrong. And even as open war was declared by Britain and France they had the baffling satisfaction of seeing Poland fall to their armies with scarcely more than a trifling effort. The High Command faced their Supreme Commander sheepishly, fearful of his intuitions. Where next would they lead?

Below: The British declare war. Would they help Poland? *Right:* The Führer. A flattering portrait by Hoffmann

The General in action

Though the fate of Poland was to all intents and purposes sealed within a few hours of the *coup* of 1st September, acknowledged defeat was delayed until the 27th, ten days after the government had interned itself in Rumania. On that day Warsaw surrendered after devastating air and artillery attacks. Like cats glutted with cream the two 'victorious' nations claimed that there was no longer anything to fight for:

'After the definite settlement of the problems arising from the collapse of the Polish state it will serve the true interest of all peoples to put an end to the state of war existing between Germany on the one hand and England and France on the other.'

Thus Ribbentrop and Molotov as the joint mouthpiece of Hitler. It was a worthless peace offer, no more than a façade of good intentions. Hitler had already secretly declared to the High Command his determination to crush Russia, as we have seen. Peace in the West would have suited that purpose, certainly, and to sue for it was a politically sound move since it gave the impression that his territorial demands truly were ended and that he was aggrieved rather than aggressive. ('Hitler's Peace offer – No War Aims Against Britain and France – Reduction of Armaments – Peace Conference' – the headlines shrieked from the *Völkischer Beobachter;* and when Chamberlain and Daladier rejected the hollow offer even bigger type announced 'Britain Chooses War'.) But all such overtures were no more than attempts at self-vindication. Now that they had been sniffily turned down Hitler's larger designs could be pursued. 'I am determined to act aggressively and without much delay', he said on 9th October in Directive No. 6. Russia, soothed with a peace-and-trade pact and half of Poland as a material prize, could wait while Western Europe was dealt with.

Strategically, Britain and France had played into Hitler's hands. Much of the enormous French army was

Hitler with Admiral Raeder

68

cringing in the Maginot Line; the British Expeditionary Force under Lord Gort tardily arrived in France during the autumn and winter. The two Allies had manoeuvred themselves into the position of being bound by treaty to aid Poland. Now, with Poland overcome in a débacle they sat glumly wondering what to do next. With more than a hundred divisions of French soldiers spread across France and Hitler's effective strength concentrated in Poland throughout September and well into October, the Allies sat and paused to consider their course of action, if any.

Hitler did not wonder what to do next. Conveniently for him, part of the BEF straddled the River Lys along the Franco-Belgian frontier. An excuse was thus ready made to overrun France to 'prevent the clear intention of the British and French forces to invade the Low Countries' – a typically Hitlerian gambit.

His generals, well aware of their military weakness everywhere except in Poland, and again basing their strategy on what Hitler described as 'outmoded and weak notions', saw no sense in extending a war that could well be triumphantly concluded by compromise if the Franco-British defensive enemy were not forced into action. They produced excuse after excuse for inaction: the coming winter, the impregnability of the Maginot Line, doubts whether the forces in Poland could be re-equipped and transferred to the West, the huge losses that would have to be faced . . . Their excuses were, to be sure, based largely on conventional military thought; but there was too an underlying distrust of their Führer's leadership. His ruthlessness had too often been expressed in extreme forms of violence toward those who opposed him – as in the purge of June 1934. The distrust led to conspiratorial designs on his life. One of them appeared to be within a streak of success when a

Poland. *Above left*: Hitler watches troops cross the frontier, 1st September 1939.
Above and *below*: Victory parade through Warsaw

Above: General Brauchitsch.
Right: The scuttled Graf Spee on fire off Montevideo

bomb exploded in the hall in Munich where he was speaking on 8th November 1939, but turned out to be a carefully arranged Gestapo plot to enable him to say 'Now I am certain! The fact that I left the hall before the Communist bomb exploded is a corroboration that Providence intends me to reach my goal'. Providence intended nothing of the sort, as we now know; but the opposition among the generals was stiffened by the event. By that time, though, Hitler had ordered that the attack in the West should begin on 12th November.

It did not so begin. The Führer was cunning enough to allow himself to accept the advice of his army Commander-in-chief, Walter von Brauchitsch, and Franz Halder, his Chief-of-Staff, to delay the attack because of the winter weather. He saw that by doing so he would later be able to throw their incompetence in their faces and use it to justify his refusal to be influenced by them any further. Though he pretended to accept their

advice, a winter attack in the West did not accord with his intuition, in spite of the urgency with which he had pressed for it. His megalomania was becoming intense and had been fed by the sweeping success in Poland. He was determined to see another débâcle. And with Britain still hurriedly preparing for a war her negligent attitude had ensured would overtake her, there could be no débâcle. Regulars, Territorials and conscripts forming the BEF were still lacking arms and equipment when war was declared. As they arrived in France and took up defensive positions along the Maginot Line and the Belgian frontier, it was clear to Hitler that they were scarcely worth the effort of an all-out attack. But in Britain conscription and training were proceeding more or less smoothly and production of war material was getting into its stride. By the spring there would be on the continent of Europe a British force worthy of defeat. He could afford to wait. 'It may

cost me a million men', he told Ernst Weizäcker, Secretary in the Foreign Office, 'but it will cost the enemy that too – and the enemy cannot stand it'.

Meanwhile, his most effective blows could be aimed at sea power; so throughout the winter of 1939-40 – the period that by its inactivity became called 'the phoney war' – it was the Navy that did the fighting. The pocket battleship *Graf Spee* sank nine British merchantmen before she was brought to battle on 13th December and pursued to the River Plate, where she scuttled herself. Earlier, German submarines had sunk the Battleship *Royal Oak* in Scapa Flow, and the armed merchant cruiser *Rawalpindi* had been sunk in battle against the *Scharnhorst* and *Gneisenau* in November. But even at sea there were no spectacular engagements. 'It seems as if the rape of Poland has knocked both sides into shocked inanition', one of the neutral newspapers of the Irish Republic said with surprising credulity and dubious semantics.

Hitler's 'inanition' was by no means shocked. Nor was it inanition. He was carefully planning an operation which he saw as essential if the western powers were to be completely defeated – the invasion of Norway.

That design was one of the outstanding examples of his generalship. To control the long Norwegian coast with its innumerable harbours and fjords would give him naval and aircraft bases for attacks against Allied shipping in the North Atlantic. To counteract those attacks, British and French sea and air forces would have to be drawn off from other vital areas – for example the Mediterranean and North Sea; and Hitler was particularly interested in the vulnerability of the Mediterranean, since to dominate it was to open the gateway to French possessions in North Africa. There was also to be considered the great material advantage of gaining control of Norway's immense output of iron ore. Denied to the enemy, the lack of that vital commodity could

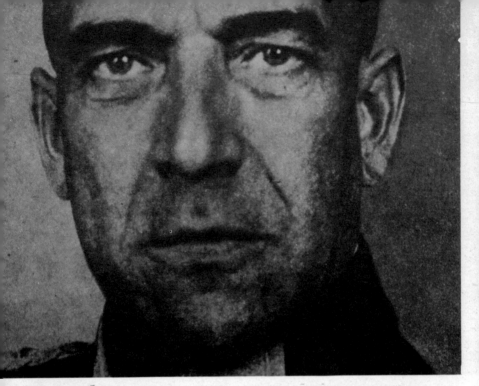

make a significant difference to their armaments production.

The conception of the Norwegian campaign was claimed by Hitler as his own. True, the German naval archives reveal that Admiral Raeder suggested, at a conference on 10th October 1939, that the capture of Norwegian bases would enable him to challenge British naval supremacy; but 'the Führer cast the suggestion aside furiously' – a reaction that was psychologically in key. He was responding characteristically to the attempted wrenching from him by one of his High Command of a cherished idea. It was a brilliant idea and Hitler knew it. He did not intend to let any credit for it elude him. He took it as an affront that Raeder should innocently have come up with an idea that was already, so to speak, in the portfolio of his intuitive design for the conduct of the war. To cast Raeder's suggestion furiously aside was therefore merely the blustering attempt of a man of unstable temperament, caught off his

The Norwegian campaign. *Above:* Falkenhorst, the German commander. *Right:* Infantry advance outside Oslo

guard, to prevent the reins of control being taken from his hands.

'Before I became Chancellor', he had said to justify his arrogation of supreme power, 'I thought the General Staff was like a mastiff which had to be held tight by the collar because it threatened all and sundry. Since then I have to recognize that the General Staff is anything but that. It has consistently tried to impede every action I have thought necessary. It is I who have always had to goad on this mastiff'.

The General Staff were for the time being kept completely in the dark about the Norwegian operation, since he could hardly reject Raeder's suggestion and then be seen to adopt it. It was in fact unnecessary that they should know. 'Why should I demoralize my enemy by military means if I can do so better and more cheaply

in other ways?' Hitler had written in
Mein Kampf. The 'other ways' were,
in the case of Norway, the estab-
lishment of Vidkun Quisling's Fifth
Column of Nazi sympathizers. 'Hitler
knew', Major-General Fuller has said,
'that in a democratic country an
army is next to useless should the
people sympathize with the enemy . . .
which is why in autocratically ruled
countries their governments raise
two armies, one to fight their enemies
and the other to control their peoples'.

Quisling, like Hitler, was a bitter
and fearful opponent of Communism
and had, so to speak, prostrated
himself before the German leader.
His obeisances were not without self-
interest. He hoped to carve out a
career as Führer of Norway. The
party he had formed to follow him,
which he called *Nasjonal Samling*
(National Unity), had been contemptuously treated by the electorate and
gained only two per cent of the votes
and no seat in the parliament.
Secretly dismayed by that response

he had nonetheless used his army
connexions – he was a major and had
been Military Attaché in Moscow – to
disseminate Nazi ideas among the
forces. Those attempts had had considerable success: Hitler's ceaseless
drumming up of the military virtues
of the Nordic races had not been
without its propaganda effect.

So, when the war began, Quisling
went to see Hitler in Berchtesgaden to
discuss the affairs of the Thule
Society, an organization which used
Nordic mythology as a cover for its
surreptitious political activities. The
affairs discussed on this occasion were
the tactics of the *Nasjonal Samling.*
Hitler himself wrote down what were
to be that Party's aims. These were:
to restrict British naval power by
establishing naval and air bases on
the west coast of Norway; to lie
athwart the sea communications
between Britain and Northern Russia;
to open the North Sea and the Atlantic
to the German fleet; and to secure the
sea route for the shipping of iron ore

to Germany. Quisling's help in these undercover activities was to be rewarded with leadership of the Norwegian government as soon as the invasion had proved successful. (His ultimate reward was to have Hitler's memorandum produced in evidence against him at his trial for treason in October 1945.)

Having indulged in a great deal of mutual soft-soaping, Führer and quasi-Führer parted. Hitler had recognized in his henchman a strain of megalomania. It was of a lesser virulence than his own and therefore could be twisted into subservience; but it must be watched. 'Quisling', he later told Himmler, 'must be discredited as soon as he has served his purpose. In no circumstances must he be allowed power of other than secondary value'. For the time being, though, the carrot was before the donkey – a Trojan donkey who could safely be left to organize half the battle for Norway.

Thus, quite apart from Hitler's reluctance to allow any real strategic power to fall into the hands of his General Staff, it was in the case of the Norwegian campaign unnecessary. All that was needed in Germany was the intensive training of Austrian troops in mountain warfare, and that was put in hand immediately, their commander, General von Falkenhorst, being given only the sketchiest notion of the venue of his forthcoming expedition – though as an experienced soldier he can hardly have been bereft of ideas on that subject.

Meanwhile, Hitler continued to prevaricate, and to seem to allow himself to be influenced by the High Command and General Staff, whose insistent advice was to delay the attack in the West.

Meanwhile also, the Russians had set about invading Finland with a vast superiority of numbers which they gleefully assumed would bring that tiny country to her knees in a

Left: Quisling (civilian clothes) with German officers. *Above:* Hitler, Keitel, and Mannerheim

matter of days and give her mighty conqueror the port of Hangö for a naval base, which Russia dearly wanted. There was no easy conquest however. Superior though the Russians were in numbers – they had a hundred divisions against the Finns' three – they were unbelievably incompetent in organization and strategy. The Finns' resistance – they were led by Field-Marshal Mannerheim – kept the enemy at bay from 30th November 1939 to 10th March 1940 and inflicted grievous losses on the Russian forces. In the end it was simply brute force, the indiscriminate throwing into battle of thousands of Russian troops and airmen, that made Finland surrender to Marshal Timoshenko's hordes. Great noises of self-righteous triumph were voiced abroad in the party organ *Pravda,* but

it was clear that Russian morale had been lowered to near zero by a campaign that had been extended, by the Finns' superiority, from the expected three days to more than three months.

To no-one was it more clear than Hitler. Brooding upon his declared intention 'to crush the Soviet Union', he confided to Keitel, his Chief of Staff, that 'the moral defeat of Communist Russia at the hands of a tiny country like Finland proves unequivocally that she stands no chance at all against the organized might of the Reich'. In the circumstances it was a reasonable judgement. But, as he was to find to his cost, he had not taken into account the fact that more effective lessons are learned from defeats than from victories. The Russians learned theirs in Finland.

The period of the phoney war ended in April 1940 with the rapid and complete success of the Norwegian invasion. Quisling's Fifth Column methods proved invaluable. His trait-

The Russo-Finnish war of 1939. Soviet troops occupy Viborg, October 1939

ors occupied Oslo and aided the German airborne troops who landed there. Seaborne troops were stowed into the holds of merchant vessels which sailed up the Kattegat to Oslo to complete the occupation of the capital. Denmark was invaded on the same day (9th April) and capitulated without resistance, having been given a pledge by Hitler that her political independence would be respected. (Needless to say, it wasn't.) By nightfall all the key points of Norway – Oslo, Kristiansund, Trondheim, Bergen, Stavanger – were in Falkenhorst's hands.

The campaign was seen by many in Britain to be an act of madness. Churchill – at that time First Lord of the Admiralty – said, 'I consider that Hitler's action in invading Scandinavia is as great a strategic and political error as that which was committed by Napoleon in 1807 when he invaded Spain . . . I feel that we are greatly advantaged by what has occurred, provided we turn to the utmost profit the strategic blunder into which our mortal enemy has been provoked.'

Far from turning the occasion to the utmost profit, delays and muddle resulted in nothing more than the heroic but useless attempt to wrest power from the Germans by combined sea and air attacks on the ports of Trondheim, Aandalsnes, Narvik and Namos. These did not begin till 15th April, by which time the enemy was firmly rooted in all key centres. In any case the naval and air forces' efforts were so poorly integrated that the landing of troops in the fjords

and let us have done with you. In the name of God, go!' Two days later Chamberlain resigned and Churchill became Prime Minister. That much at least had been achieved.

It now became very clear that far from being an act of madness Hitler's first blow since the declaration of war had been timed perfectly. For it was followed almost immediately by his second. 'The morning of 10th May dawned', Churchill recorded in his history of the war, 'and with it came tremendous news. Boxes with telegrams poured in from the Admiralty, the War Office, and the Foreign Office. The Germans had struck their long-awaited blow. Holland and Belgium were both invaded. Their frontiers had been crossed at numerous points. The whole movement of the German army upon the invasion of the Low Countries and of France had begun.'

Hitler's 'justification' for pouring his armies into Belgium and Holland was, as before, 'to prevent the clear intention of Britain and France to invade defenceless territory'. His timing continued to be perfect. There was now, in France, a BEF worth attacking. It consisted of seven regiments of light tanks, a regiment of armoured cars of antiquated design, two battalions of infantry tanks (their 'armament' was a single machine gun), and thirteen infantry divisions of which three could scarcely be counted since they had no artillery to support them and only vestigial transport to move them. The BEF's entire backing from the air was from one fighter and one bomber wing of the Royal Air Force, and its lines of communication were excessively long, stretching as they did to Le Havre, Brest and Nantes. The fighting quality of the Force lay almost entirely in its men. Its armour was feeble almost to the point of uselessness; it was underequipped and vulnerable to air attack. But its defeat would be a punishing blow to the Allies.

Hitler also had, as he very well

could not be accomplished quickly enough, and German bombing attacks could not be dealt with by British fighters because all the aerodromes were in German hands. (A crazy scheme to land a Squadron of planes on a frozen lake near Dombaas ended inevitably in their destruction.) The attempt having been doomed from the start, the Allied Supreme War Council shook themselves like shaggy dogs and decided to withdraw all troops from central Norway on 27th April, leaving a sprinkling in the north to deal with Narvik.

The lamentable conduct of the Norwegian affair resulted in the voicing in Westminster of the opinion of the country in general when Mr L S Amery quoted Cromwell's words to the Long Parliament: 'You have sat too long here for any good you have been doing. Depart, I say,

Left: Churchill, as First Lord of the Admiralty, in nautical rig. *Above:* Norwegians defending Narvik. *Below:* After the British bombardment of Narvik

Manstein, author of the German plan for the invasion of France

Gamelin, French Commander-in-Chief

knew, the French armies to contend with. There were 102 divisions. Forty of them were stretched out from the English Channel to the Maginot Line; twenty-six were in the Line itself; and thirty-six were lined up facing the Alpes Maritimes. They had of course been there all the time. It was a complete mystery to the German General Staff that they had not moved since the war began. General Siegfried Westphal says in *The German Army in the West*:

'Every expert serving at that time [September 1939] in the Western Army felt his hair standing on end when he considered the possibility of an immediate French attack. It was incomprehensible that no such attack should take place, that the appalling weakness of the German defence should be unknown to the French leaders. If the French had thrown the weight of their forces into an offensive in September 1939 they would have been able to reach the Rhine in two weeks. The German forces immediately available in the West were much too weak to block the path of a French assault or even threaten seriously the flanks of the attacking wedge. Naturally units could have been withdrawn rapidly from Poland and transferred

to the West, but nevertheless the French and British air forces should have found it possible to damage the lines of communication inside Germany sufficiently to slow down this process. The theme of every General Staff exercise ... had been the beating-off of a French attack by the German Army of which parts had to be retained in the East because of . . . Poland. In each of these exercises the French broke out of the narrow space of less than two hundred kilometres between the Mosel and the Rhine, later proceeding along the northern bank of the Mosel and finally crossing the Upper Rhine in the region of Karlsruhe. In every case they had been able to penetrate to the Rhine in the course of a few weeks, even though it was assumed that a much greater number of divisions, and in particular the majority of the active ones, were taking part in the German defence.'

Though it was incomprehensible to the German General Staff that no attack had been made by the Allies in September, it was no mystery to Hitler. He had contemptuously watched the exercises that were based on the premise of a French breakthrough at Karlsruhe and remarked to Jodl, chief of the Wehrmacht control staff,

'The French were obsessed with defence in 1920; they are obsessed with defence still. They are like a rabbit facing a stoat; they cannot move for fear.'

His own army, he considered, seemed to be fatally conventional. 'I have the greatest contempt for orthodoxy when it can lead only to feeble ideas. The General Staff will strangle themselves with their orthodoxy'. He had been willing to let them do so between the autumn of 1939 and the spring of 1940, accepting their excuses for delaying the attack in the West with a pretended patience that conveniently disguised his alarm that his intuition about the spinelessness of the French might be wrong. But he was not wrong. 'The side which stays within its fortifications is beaten.' Now that he had secured Norway with an impeccably performed set-piece, the French had certified themselves as flabby and stupid, and the British had as usual pushed their Expeditionary Force over to France with great conscientiousness and no apparent object – now was the time to trigger off the plan that had been in the making throughout the winter. Hence the spate of dispatches that astonished Mr Churchill – and everybody else, seemingly – on the morning of 10th May.

There were two Commands between Hitler and his forces: his own, the OKW, Supreme Command of all the Armed Forces, and the OKH, the ordinary Army High Command. This last was the computer that worked out the details of his grand designs. The OKH's original plan for attack in the West was, as Hitler had said, uninspired. It was to repeat the German action of 1914, with a right wing sweeping movement through Belgium and Holland, a centre opposite the Ardennes, and a left wing facing what was now the Maginot Line. The result would have been entirely predictable, since the French also would have been thinking in First World War terms – had in fact based their plan, such as it was, on that very method of attack.

Paul Reynaud, French Prime Minister, on the eve of war

An alternative scheme had been worked out and proposed by Field-Marshal von Rundstedt's Chief of Staff, General von Manstein. He thought that the main thrust should be made through the Ardennes, since that area was weakly defended – the French believing in their innocence that it was too densely forested for tanks to operate in. Hitler at once saw the possibilities of such a plan; but as with Raeder's proposal for Norway he had no intention of appearing to be malleable in the hands of his generals. It was February before he allowed himself to be 'persuaded'; but thenceforth he implemented the scheme relentlessly, in the face of such opposition as the OKH put forward on the ground that it was too risky. He not only ordered its implementation but – repeating his behaviour with Raeder – adopted it as his own. 'My plan will result in a lightning victory', he told Halder at the conference on the morning of 9th May when the final order to begin the attack – there had been sixteen earlier orders and counter-orders – was given.

He can scarcely be said to have been unwarrantably optimistic. By the afternoon of the 10th Holland was overrun. 'The Dutch Ministers were

in my room', Churchill writes. 'Haggard and worn, with horror in their eyes, they had just flown over from Amsterdam. Their country had been attacked without the slightest pretext of warning. The avalanche of fire and steel had rolled across the frontiers, and when resistance broke out and the Dutch frontier guards fired an overwhelming onslaught was made from the air. The whole country was in a state of wild confusion. The long-prepared defence scheme had been put into operation; the dykes were opened, the waters spread far and wide. But the Germans had already crossed the outer lines, and were now streaming down the banks of the Rhine and through the inner Grave-lines defences.'

Two days later the main thrust – forty-four divisions, including a column of armour over a hundred miles long – crossed the Ardennes and the French frontier and were over the River Meuse on the 13th. Its advance was phenomenally quick. There was virtually nothing to oppose it but a couple of divisions of second-rate

Above: The 'impenetrable' Maginot line falls to the Germans. *Right:* Hitler and Göring gleeful after the defeat of France

French troops, elderly reservists who were more or less immobile for lack of transport and had only one anti-tank gun per kilometre of front. Along the whole line Louvain – Namur – Dinant – Sedan, where the rest of the French Ninth Army had been deployed, a battle developed in which the French troops were liquidated by the advancing tanks of General von Kleist and the wickedly effective dive-bombing of Göring's Stukas. General Gamelin, who was the Commander-in-Chief of all the Allied armies sent a dumbfounded message to Churchill: 'I am surprised and alarmed at the speed and power of the enemy's advance'. Pathetic creature. He had every reason to be alarmed. His 'Plan D' had been designed to face a German attack in September 1939, when the bulk of the German army was engaged in Poland. It had not been altered one whit in the eight months since,

Preis 20
5. Dezember
Nummer 49 /
Druck und Ver
DuMont Sch
Auslandspreise siehe

Kölnische
Illustrierte Zeitung

...denkampf
unserer zerst...
...RTSETZUNG DES GROSSEN NARVIK-BERIC...

**Freude
über den Sieg!**

...a bisher nicht veröffent-
...htes Bild des Führers
...d des Reichsmarschalls
...genommen nach der
...zösischen Kapitulation

...victoire décisive comme la
...la plus intense! / Photo
...graphie inédite représentant
...Führer et le Maréchal du
...ch immédiatement après la
...capitulation de la France

Left and *above:* **Victorious Germans pass the Arc de Triomphe, Paris, May 1940**

despite the frequent observations of the British Chiefs of Staff that the German army was growing in strength every day and that its tactics would not necessarily be those of 1914. Gamelin was an out-dated old buffer who had been expected to retire on the outbreak of war and hand over command of the French and British armies to General Georges. He could not bear to relinquish his authority, however; and now that his rickety arrangements had proved disastrous he came bleating to Churchill for help – 'Ten more squadrons of fighters'.

Churchill had no fighters to give him. On the morning of the 15th the French Prime Minister, Paul Reynaud, telephoned him reproachfully. 'We have been defeated. We are beaten. We have lost the battle'. Churchill could not believe it. He promised to

fly to Paris and talk, rather as a parent comforts a terrified child in a storm. He arrived at the Quai d'Orsay at 5.30 the same afternoon. His first words to Gamelin after he had heard a run-down of the situation and understood the sinister significance of the Ardennes breakthrough were: 'Where is the strategic reserve?' Gamelin replied that there was none. Thinking he had misunderstood the question Churchill put it in French. *'Ou est la masse de manoeuvre?'* And again Gamelin replied, *'Aucune'*.

Now it was Churchill's turn to be dumbfounded. 'What were we to think of the great French Army and its highest chiefs? It had never occurred to me that any commanders having to defend five hundred miles of engaged front would have left themselves unprovided with a strategic reserve. No-one can defend with certainty so wide a front; but when the enemy has committed himself to a major thrust which breaks the line one can always have, one *must* always have, a mass of divisions which marches up in vigorous counterpoint at the moment when the first fury of the offensive has spent its force.

'What was the Maginot Line for? It should have economized troops upon a large section of the frontier, not only offering many sally-ports for local counter-strokes, but also enabling large forces to be held in reserve; and this is the only way these things can be done. But now there was no reserve. I admit this was one of the greatest surprises I have had in my life. Why had I not known more about it, even though I had been so busy at the Admiralty? Why had the British Government, and the War Office above all, not known more about it?'

He might well have asked. Two years later the same baffled Churchill was to ask the same question about the lack of defences in Singapore. The simple answer in both cases was that he assumed, mistakenly, that those responsible were fit for their jobs. The enemy knew better.

Hitler's prophecy of a lightning victory was fulfilled. Within a month the tremendous impetus of the German advance had resulted, *seriatim*, in the surrender of Holland, the surrender of Belgium, the evacuation from Dunkirk of 337,131 men of the BEF who had been trapped between Rundstedt's forces advancing from the south and General von Bock's advancing from the north, and the German occupation of Paris. The French Government fled to Bordeaux on 14th June. The aged Marshal Pétain succeeded Reynaud as head of the Government and his immediate task was to seek an armistice. It was the end of the Third Republic.

The Führer managed the armistice with a stroke of malicious drama. He ordered that it should be signed in the famous railway sleeping-car in which the 1918 armistice had been signed. The car stood as a museum piece at Réthondes in the Forest of Compiègne beside the stone on which was engraved the memorial 'Here on the eleventh of November 1918 succumbed the criminal pride of the German empire, vanquished by the free peoples which it tried to enslave.' William Shirer, the War Correspondent, who was present, says, 'To dictate an armistice in this historic place was sweet revenge for the man who had been a lowly corporal in the army which had been forced to give up in 1918, and he did not hide his feelings. Standing a few feet away, I saw his face light up, successively, with hate, scorn, revenge, triumph . . .'

For a few moments he stood thus in the coach; then he marched out into the sunny clearing, leaving Keitel to read the preamble to the declaration – a declaration that Hitler himself had written, and which was 'to efface once and for all by an act of reparative justice a memory . . . which was resented by the German people as the greatest shame of all time'.

The Pact of Steel. Sometimes it nearly collapsed

General Keitel, for once, answers Hitler back

Lest it be assumed that Hitler watched with icy calm or tranquil smile as his armies swept through Europe, let that impression be corrected at once. Hitler was no Wellington – though like the great General of Waterloo, his army leaders had so far proved to be better than his opponents'. But their quality owed nothing whatever to him. Nor did he exactly encourage their tolerance.

Throughout his infamous career from nonentity to Führer of the Third Reich there had been stormy scenes whenever events fell out badly or his generals ran counter to him in their proposals, and often when they didn't. His petulance was sometimes masked by a deceptive oiliness – 'the smile on the face of the tiger' – when he planned the obliteration of anyone who threatened to undermine his authority. (He had invited Röhm to tea on the afternoon of 4th June 1934 and was 'excessively cheerful and friendly' while planning the purge of the 30th, in which Röhm was shot after receiving a letter from the Führer thanking him for his 'imperishable services'.) But all his generals testify in their diaries and other records to the scenes of rage that so frequently formed the backdrop to the 'conferences' at which the schemes of war were propounded. Halder, for example, on 18th May 1940:

'Führer keeps worrying about south flank. He rages and screams that we are on the way to ruin the whole campaign. He won't have any part in continuing the operation in a westward direction'.

And, earlier, Weizäcker on the eve of war:

'He grew more and more excited and began to wave his arms as he shouted in my face:

'"If England wants to fight for a year, I shall fight for a year; if England wants to fight two years I shall fight two years." He paused and then yelled, his voice rising to a shrill scream and his arms milling wildly. "If England wants to fight for three years I shall fight for three years.'' The movements of his body now began to follow those of his arms, and when he finally bellowed ''And if necessary I will fight for ten years'' he brandished his fist and bent down so that it nearly touched the floor. The situation was highly embarrassing, so embarrassing in fact that Göring reacted perceptibly to the spectacle Hitler was making of himself by turning on his heel so that he had his back to both of us.'

That outburst – very typical – was merely Hitler's response to a suggestion by Weizäcker that England might be readier to fight than he had contemptuously implied.

There were occasions too when bewilderment seemed to overcome him as he contemplated the inevitable results of his actions, as if an unfair blow had been struck at him by fate. One such occasion was the reading to him, by his interpreter Paul Schmidt, of the British ultimatum on the morning of 3rd September 1939. Schmidt writes:

'Hitler was sitting at his desk and Ribbentrop stood by the window. Both looked up expectantly as I came in. I stopped at some distance from Hitler's desk, and then slowly translated the British Government's ultimatum. When I finished there was complete silence. Hitler sat immobile, gazing before him. He was obviously at a loss, as was afterward stated, but he did not rage as others allege. He sat completely silent and unmoving. After an interval, which seemed an age, he turned to Ribbentrop, who had remained standing by the window. ''What now?'' asked Hitler with a savage look, as though implying that his Foreign Minister had misled him about England's probable reaction.'

Throughout the voluminous documentation that comments on his behaviour there is abundant evidence of his instability. It is an extension and magnification of August Kubizek's recognition of the same characteristic. But now his manic-depressive nature had been intensified by the action of *Spirochaeta pallida* on the cortex of his brain and possibly exacerbated by the drugs used to combat the disease. 'It is remarkable', Göebbels wrote in his diary in January 1940 with an unwitting finger on the heart of the matter, 'how much the Führer is becoming an enlargement of himself.'

Not only is there a veritable cornucopia of documentation of Hitler's increasing instability, but also of his militant determination to interfere with the plans of the Army High Command. Only in the Polish campaign can he be said to have left his Generals to plan and execute in detail a conquest that turned out to be triumphant. Perhaps their triumph was too much for him. From the beginning of the Norwegian campaign his megalomania forced, as Westphal says, a gulf between him 'and the German army leaders [that] was absolute and unbridgeable. It arose from the always irreconcilable conflict between concrete and abstract thinking, between sober objectivity and the chasing of fancies, between logical calculation based on facts and the attempt to force the facts to fit impossible desires . . . In the Third Reich the motto was ''Death to the expert, particularly the soldier''. Not only Hitler but almost every Party leader believed himself to possess a more soundly based judgement in all questions concerning the conduct of the war than that possessed by the leaders of the Army.'

The general can be allowed his bitterness. He was a staff officer of great distinction under Rundstedt, Kesselring and Rommel and was no dyed-in-the-wool reactionary. He saw Hitler set blood 'flowing in rivers without scruple' and recognized his foolish fear of letting the smallest control slip from his fingers as another manifestation of his instability:

'His experience was the common one of dilettanti. For a certain time they have beginner's luck; they turn out to be right where the experts were wrong; in their audacity they achieve much that the professionals could not have brought about with the same speed and ease. Then, however, in the intoxication of success, their feet leave the common ground. This happens in all walks of life and it is no different in warfare. The military layman underestimates the strength of the enemy and rates his own potentialities too highly. He sees things not as they are but as he would like to have them. He drives away all who would warn him, lest they should cast shadows over his rosy picture, and he will have none of their advice. But when the dilettante is not an average man whose absurdity is soon made apparent, but a being who holds absolute power in his hands and who is driven by demonic urges, it is far worse. For then as time goes on he rejects even that truth which he once had recognized. Even so was it with Hitler.'

There is a measure of understandable misjudgement here. To the professional all who lack his trained skill are amateurs. The 'natural' is unacceptable, his intuitions are not to be trusted. If Hitler had attained a command in the First World War he would have been, so to speak, eligible for consideration in the hierarchy; if such a command had been even in the slightest degree noteworthy he would have been acceptable; for his rantings about the 'Masonry' of the Army were not wholly unjustified. Soldiering, in Germany as in England, had always, until the inter-war period, suffered from the effects of class structure –an effect good in some ways, disastrous in others; but ineradicable. 'Soldiers', Hitler once told Goebbels, 'learn seven principles of war like a creed. They are certain that so long as they maintain the objective, keep up offensive action, surprise the enemy, economize with their forces, make good security arrangements, co-operate with their flanking formations, and concentrate on conquest, they are bound to win.

Göring, Hitler and Keitel in strategic conference, 1941

They forget that the enemy knows the same formula. They forget that battles can be half won before a shot is fired. They forget the value of the political weapon.'

But by the time of the fall of France Hitler had forced all possible advantage from the political weapon. By trick, propaganda and diplomacy he had secured his followers and his allies. (Mussolini quaveringly threw in his hand with his fellow Fascist on 10th June 1940.) The German nation was behind him – in effect in its entirety, since the Gestapo, the concentration camp and the firing squad awaited those who demurred or wandered from the ideological fold where Hitler was bellwether. He had no more to gain from the hypnotism of his presence at such gatherings as the Nuremberg rallies. The cunning of the politician needed to be tempered by the discipline of the soldier; but that was not a quality so easily wrung from a man of Hitler's stamp.

The question naturally arises, then, as to his ability as a military leader. Was his 'intuition', his psychological insight into his opponents' reactions, a valuable asset? His generals, driven frantic by his interference – unless they were virtually no more than toadying personal assistants like Jodl and Keitel – would have set little store by it. The harsh realities of military manoeuvres were to them far more important than any assessment of the character of their opponents. It was, for army men, a reasonable order of priorities. It did not follow, however, that it was *ipso facto* the right order. Used wisely, the gift of insight is of immense value in supplementing, if not instigating, a course of action. But a serious flaw lay in Hitler's inability to subjugate it to the commonsense dictates of military prerogative. It was a flaw that was to have fatal effects on his leadership.

The General in decline

Before pursuing the track of Hitler's Generalship from its zenith to its nadir, it will be as well to summarize and evaluate his achievements to date.

His first step to military power was of course to acquire theoretical overlordship of all the armed forces at the same time as he united the offices of President and Chancellor in August 1934, upon the death of Hindenberg. (This titular office of Supreme Commander was indivisible from that of Head of State.) He found, though, that he had acquired also a hornet's nest of disruptive forces. The reactionary spirit of the Officer Corps was one he was well aware of. He had seen many signs of sullen objection to his attitude to the Church, to the speed with which he was insisting on rearmament and conscription, to dangerous moves such as the reoccupation of the Rhineland, and to the infiltration of Himmler's police methods into the cherished traditions of the Corps. But there were smaller irritants that he quickly realized could be equally troublesome to him; and those he shrewdly turned to advantage as soon as opportunities presented themselves.

In particular, the personal affairs of General Werner von Blomberg, War Minister and Commander-in-Chief of all the Armed Forces, and Colonel-General Werner von Fritsch, Commander-in-Chief of the Army, proved to be an Open Sesame on the Führer's route through the labyrinth of power.

Blomberg was a weak man who had achieved high rank in the army only because he greased palms and made genuflections in the right direction at the right time. He had no special military ability. He had wormed his way into President Hindenberg's favour and had been nominated War Minister as a condition of Hitler's appointment to the Chancellorship in 1933. Hitler had expected him to be something of a thorn in his side; but

Map conference with Rundstedt. Hitler dismissed him no less than three times

as things turned out Blomberg had, by his vacillating nature, been a valuable link between the upstart Chancellor and the rigidly reactionary Officer Corps. Hitler, in 1933 altogether uncertain of holding on to the power he had achieved largely by chance, shrewdly cultivated the acquaintance of the man who could chamfer away the Army's resentment.

Then, at the end of 1937, Blomberg decided to get married and asked Hitler to act as a witness at the wedding. Himmler, however, had looked into the affianced lady's past. The search had proved rewarding. Heydrich, Himmler's chief of intelligence had produced a dossier recording forty-two convictions for prostitution against Fraülein Erna Grühn. Even more titillating was a file of obscene photographs for which the War Minister's intended had posed. Himmler arranged for a surreptitious leakage of this interesting information and also brought it to Hitler's attention. The Führer, genuinely outraged by Blomberg's indiscretion and his seeming endorsement of the liaison, insisted upon the War Minister's resignation.

His natural successor was the Army Commander-in-Chief, Fritsch, but Hitler's and Himmler's long-term interests demanded that the automatic succession of generals to War Ministry should cease. It was therefore very convenient that the Gestapo was able to produce an even more damaging. dossier against Fritsch, which portrayed him as a practising homosexual. He also produced a male prostitute who had been bribed or bullied into identifying Fritsch as a former client. All this was a farrago of his (the evidence in fact related to a retired Captain Frisch, as Himmler and the Gestapo well knew) but the atmosphere of crisis robbed Frisch's explanations of conviction. He was sent on leave and though eventually cleared by a Court of Honour, never reinstated.

Having thus removed two obstacles

from his path Hitler announced to the Cabinet on 4th February that he himself would now become Commander-in-Chief of all the Armed Forces. That is, he assumed Supreme Command in a practical as well as a titular sense. The War Ministry would be abolished and its place taken by the OKW – the *Oberkommando der Wehrmacht,* or High Command of all the Armed Forces, with the yes-man General Wilhelm Keitel at its administrative head and at Hitler's right hand. Brauchitsch would be made Commander-in-Chief of the Army, Göring would be a Field-Marshal and the senior officer of all the forces, and more than a dozen other generals of whose loyalty Hitler was extremely doubtful would be transferred to the retired list.

Thus, by way of events that he had not even precipitated himself, Hitler undermined the power of the Officer Corps and by the same token ensured that he was actual as well as titular director of all the armed forces. The Head of State, moving warily, had reinforced his power as dictator with those of general. That was his most valuable achievement, since without it none of his later ones could have been attempted, let alone implemented.

There followed in the autumn of that same year, 1938, the ominous seizure of the Sudetenland – morally assisted by the Allies, which made it, perhaps, a second-rate achievement; and, a year later still, the brilliant political stroke of the agreement with the Soviet Union that held the Russians at bay while Poland was dealt with in a campaign in which, for the last time, Hitler's generals were left alone to make their own plans. The political experiment of a war localized to Poland failed, but the military one of non-interference in the professionals' strategy was too successful for Hitler's increasing megalomania and determined him to plan and direct future campaigns himself. It was a grave error.

Norway, though, hid its effects for

Hitler's variant, 'Barbarossa': the capture of Leningrad is stipulated as essential before the subsequent – and conclusive – drive on Moscow

In apparent harmony, Hitler and (right to left) Fritsch, Blomberg and Göring watch manoeuvres

the time being; and when that subtly planned and cheaply accomplished campaign was succeeded by the fall of France and the Low Countries and the débâcle of Dunkirk it was evident – anyway to him – that his own and others' utterances about his being a God-sent saviour, the choice of Providence, et cetera, had been the solemn truth. 'The effect of cerebral syphilis on a nature already afflicted with megalomania', the venereologist Anwyl-Davies has said, 'is always to increase confidence that every kind of opposition can be overcome, to see the path ahead lighted by Messianic triumphs when in fact ruinous disasters lurk in the shadows.'

To Hitler, his next step was clear. He did not underestimate the British characteristic of dogged resistance; nor did he mistakenly assume that his enemy would easily submit to the humiliation of Dunkirk. 'They will turn and snap like terriers', he told Brauchitsch. Brauchitsch sharply reminded him that Rundstedt's encircling armour, ordered to cut off and destroy the British forces heading for Dunkirk, had been stopped by Hitler's own last-minute command from completing their task. Furiously, Hitler dared Brauchitsch to question the wisdom of his direction. From the heart of the storm of abuse Brauchitsch grasped the notion that Hitler had deliberately intended the British to escape from Dunkirk so that the chances of suing for peace with them could be improved. This may have been Hitler's vague intention to begin with; but in fact it was Rundstedt himself who pointed out to Hitler that it was 'necessary to save the armour for further operations' and who stopped the encirclement movement with the Führer's agreement. Hitler was therefore right to expect the escaped enemy to 'turn and snap like terriers'.

All the same, he evidently had a half conviction that there might be an approach for peace, for on 21st May, when the continuing withdrawal of British forces made their retreat to the sea (or their annihilation in Rundstedt's pincer grip) virtually certain, Hitler had warned Admiral Raeder that the Navy's plan for the invasion of Britain 'was exceptionally difficult and must in any case be shelved' while he considered 'more urgent matters'. Whether those more urgent matters were self-reproaches for permitting the Dunkirk escape or pauses in which he hoped overtures for peace would fall cannot now be established.

As for the invasion plan, of which nothing whatever had been discussed in any of the Führer's planning conferences until now, it was a routine draft that had been made as soon as Britain had declared war and had been reposing in the German Admiralty unaltered ever since. It was no more than an embryo and had taken no account of any possibility but that of a straightforward naval fleet bombarding the south coast and ferrying troops across the English Channel at its narrowest point. Raeder's enquiry on 21st May had been merely to ascertain whether Hitler wanted the plan developed in greater detail. A month later, with no sign of any white flag appearing on the ramparts of an embattled Britain, Raeder pressed the question again, and again Hitler appeared sceptical. He was, however, sure in his own mind that the next step must be to mount the invasion. (No doubt his scepticism disguised his usual reluctance to admit anybody else's ideas as practical.) His change of heart was confirmed by two directives, the first issued on 2nd July:

'The Führer has decided that under certain conditions – the most important of which must be the achievement of the Luftwaffe's superiority in the air – an invasion of England may take place.'

The second, dated 16th July, said

'Since England in spite of her militarily hopeless position shows no sign of coming to terms, I have decided to prepare an invasion plan against England and if necessary carry it out. The preparations for this plan must be completed by mid-August'.

At a conference five days later he told the army, navy and air force chiefs that there was a 'possibility of a change in political relations with Russia'. (Since the services chiefs already knew his intentions toward Russia, which had not changed, this is a somewhat mystic comment. Presumably he referred to the superficially good relationship with Russia still extant and implied that it would not be long before his true intention was made manifest by invasion in the East. This would coincide with the strategical decision to deal with England first and thus ensure his ability to concentrate all his forces on the Russian front.) Because of the possibility of political change the invasion of England – code-named 'Sea Lion' – was to be regarded as the most effective way of concluding the war in the West first.

'But even though the distance is short', he warned the services chiefs – who can scarcely have been surprised by the information – 'this is the crossing of a sea that is dominated by the enemy. It is not a one-crossing affair, as in Norway; operational surprise cannot be expected; a defensively prepared and utterly determined enemy faces us and dominates the sea area we must use. For the Army forty divisions will be required. The most difficult part will be the material reinforcements and stores. We cannot count on supplies of any kind being available to us in England. Nor can we afford anything but complete mastery of the air. And this must be linked with a full appreciation of the weather situation. The time of year is the most important factor, for the weather in the North Sea and the Channel during the end of September is bad, and fogs begin by mid-October. The main invasion must therefore be completed by 15th September.'

The generals had learned to control their resentment when their Führer infuriatingly told them obvious facts that they were paid to know and knew. Similarly they hesitated to tell him, when the time came, that if he wanted his Luftwaffe to attain aerial mastery there was so far no prospect of attaining it in the Battle of Britain.

That attempt at mastery had begun in full force on 10th July and six weeks later had not achieved its object, which, militarily speaking, was the creation of complete confusion in London and the cutting off of all communication with the threatened south coast so that the invasion forces would land in conditions so chaotic that the defenders would stand little chance of survival. Far from achieving mastery of the air, Göring's Luftwaffe was in fact facing disastrous losses; and as August went by and Raeder's Naval Staff were showing signs of edginess because they were unable to get on with their protective mine laying in the Channel without the air cover they had been promised, the vital co-operation between the three services diminished. At the same time doubts about the Channel weather increased. So did doubts about defeating the Royal Air Force. In short, Hitler had made a tactical blunder by allowing Rundstedt to let the British escape at Dunkirk in the hope of securing a quick cheap peace; and his generals had mistimed and muddled the follow-up invasion, which no amount of tinkering could now make successful. The axiom of war that one should always reinforce success but never failure had proved to be true.

By the middle of September 'Sea

Blomberg. *Below:* With the service chiefs, Fritsch, Göring and Raeder, he salutes the Führer. *Right:* Lined up with Nazi Party worthies, 1937

Lion' had shrunk to a face-saving threat, as Raeder's report shows:

'The present air situation does not provide conditions for carrying out the operation.

'If "Sea Lion" fails it will mean a great gain in prestige for the British.

' "Sea Lion" however must not yet be cancelled, as the anxiety of the British must be kept up; if cancellation became known it would be a great relief to the British . . . [whose] main units of the Home Fleet are being held in readiness to repel the landing.

The operation remained a vague threat until February 1942, when its dusty files were finally consigned to the archives. However, no-one on either side seriously believed in it after October 1940. By that time the Battle of Britain had proved a costly failure for Göring's Luftwaffe, and the most quoted phrase in Britain was Churchill's 'Never in the field of human conflict was so much owed by so many to so few'.

Britain having successfully repelled the efforts of the Luftwaffe to reduce the capital to chaos and the rest of the country to submission, and 'Sea Lion' having failed through mis-management, Hitler lost no time in making new plans. He told his generals of them at a conference which, Halder records, was notable for its calm.

'Our efforts must now be directed to the elimination of all factors that permit England to hope for a change in the situation. Britain's hope lies in Russia and perhaps to some extent in the United States. So, if Russia drops out of the picture, America too is lost to Britain, because the elimination of Russia would greatly increase Japan's power in the Far East. Therefore: Russia's destruction must be made our next aim, and the sooner she is crushed the better. The attack will achieve its purpose only if Russia can be shattered to the roots with one blow. If we start next May [1941] we' will have five months to finish the job.

Hitler, Blomberg and Hess watch a Luftwaffe fly past

At the same time he allowed no other aspect of the war, political or military, to elude his designs. He conferred with General Franco about the possibility of Spain entering the war on Germany's side in exchange for an Axis-conquered Gibraltar, Morocco and Algeria; he got Mussolini's agreement to make no move toward the Balkans in exchange for 'the exclusive right of operations in the Mediterranean sphere'; and he connived with Pétain, who still stood feebly at the head of the defeated French government and was poisonously influenced by Pierre Laval, the traitor of Vichy, to defend the North African colonies with what was left of the French navy against British naval intervention. (France was to be rewarded with colonial possessions after a carve-up of the defeated British Empire.)

He based these designs on sound psychological reasoning. Russia he had continued to think of since the Finnish campaign as having 'no chance at all against the organized might of the Reich'. Mussolini he despised for his jealousy and fear of falling off the Axis roundabout. Franco he despised for trying to jump on it too late. To Jodl he confided that 'the Duce is acting precisely as I expected in Africa; and his troops too. We have the better part of the bargain in letting him exhaust himself there while we concern ourselves with the Rumanian oil supplies'.

The Duce, living on the glory of his 'conquest' of Abyssinia in 1936 and his crackpot notion of building a new Roman Empire, had begun his campaign in Africa in October 1940 with the blatantly trumpeted success of driving the British defence force of 2,000 out of Somaliland. To do this he had strained every nerve and flung into battle 25,000 of the 500,000 men he had concentrated in Libya, Abyssinia and Somalia. Having completed that triumph he and his Commander-in-Chief, Marshal Graziani, had sat gleefully backslapping each other while the British Navy quietly pushed through the Mediterranean a huge convoy carrying reinforcements to Egypt. With these reinforcements the campaign commander, General Wavell, achieved his great victories at Sidi Barrani and Tobruk and by the middle of January 1941 had humiliatingly defeated the Italian forces and captured 150,000 of them.

At the same time as he began the African campaign Mussolini, finding it impossible to resist interfering in the Balkans, invaded Greece through Albania; and there too the 'victorious Italian troops', as the Duce called them, were put to ignominious flight within a week.

However, pleased though Hitler might be that his despised ally had proved to be so empty of head and so flabby of heart, he was bound to assist him in order to secure German political ends; and in March 1941 one of his most experienced Generals in armoured warfare, Erwin Rommel, attacked and drove Wavell back into Egypt. 'The Führer is of the opinion', Raeder wrote in his diary, 'that it is vital for the outcome of the war that Italy does not collapse . . . It would mean a great loss of prestige for the Axis powers'.

In the Balkans too Hitler had had to assist the Duce. Greece having proved unconquerable by the Italians he had despatched some twenty divisions in early April 1941 with the object of overrunning both Yugoslavia and Greece. His alliance with Mussolini was proving extremely expensive in terms of troops. He was not without reason in his bitter reproaches against 'ungrateful and unreliable friends'.

As for Rumania, he had made his first overt moves in that direction in September 1940 by sending 'military missions [whose] tasks will be to guide friendly Rumania in organizing and instructing her forces. They will have other tasks, which must remain secret to the world, the Rumanians, and our own troops. These will be: to prepare for development from Ruman-ian bases of German forces in case a war with Soviet Russia is forced upon us, and to protect the oil district.'

The poker-faced qualification 'in case' was somewhat comical in view of Hitler's declared ambitions in the east; but it would not have surprised the Russians, who were already highly suspicious of German intentions in Rumania – and indeed elsewhere. There had been no difficulty about the partition of Poland in 1939; but with Russia and Germany trying to double-cross each other, each clinging to Rumanian oil supplies for future intentions, there was considerable resentment in Moscow when Hitler ordered eight mechanized divisions to stand by to seize the oilfields. It was a false alarm; but its effect was not mitigated by the arrival at the Kremlin of a Top Secret wire that announced that a military alliance between Germany, Italy and Japan was to be signed on 27th September 1940.

'The alliance', the Berlin wire stated with its hand on its heart, 'is directed exclusively against American warmongers. This is not expressly stated in the terms of the treaty but can be unmistakably inferred from its terms. Its exclusive purpose is to bring the elements pressing for America's entry into the war to their senses by conclusively demonstrating to them that if they enter the present struggle they will automatically have to deal with the three great powers as adversaries.'

This comforting letter was followed by a visit by Stalin's henchman, Molotov, to Berlin. At one of the conferences in the Russian Embassy he was assured that, regardless of American intervention 'no Anglo-Saxon will ever again be allowed to land on the European continent, for England is beaten and it is only a question of time before she admits her defeat'. Somewhat unfortunately the meeting had to be adjourned because of an air raid alarm and Molotov icily enquired, 'If England is defeated, why are we in an air raid shelter with

Himmler whispers pleasantries into Hitler's ear, 1938. His power is growing

British bombs falling?'

The effect of that sarcasm and of Russia's now obvious doubts and suspicions was only to arouse Hitler to uncontrollable furies frequently displayed in daily 'conferences' that should more properly be called harangues. Had Hanisch, Loffner and Neumann, the companions of his early days in Vienna, been present they would wryly have recognized the vastly magnified version of the characteristic they knew so well. His petulant and boring sounding-off about the injustices and inefficiencies of 'the system' had become a psychopathic malady that demanded that everything should be moulded to his

will. His outbursts were but the harbingers of his malice against his own army chiefs who dared to guide him, his supposed allies who dared to thwart him, and his enemies who were tougher than he expected.

In spite of the by now clearly defined turn of his mind toward insanity Hitler still had no difficulty in working out the most complex military manoeuvres. But there was a weakness in his psychological appreciations. It was to turn away from circumstantial difficulties that impinged on his intuitive assessments. For example, Franco's hesitation in throwing in his hand with the Axis because he had noted with some dismay a single day's news that Graziani's army had been routed, *HMS Illustrious* had sailed unhindered through the

Mediterranean to Egypt, and Genoa was being shelled by British warships. But though he might turn away from awkward difficulties Hitler could still at least make his assessments and believe unshakeably in their accuracy. (Such belief is of course inseparable from megalomania.) Halder records about this time that 'the Führer claims to be *always* right and at the slightest suggestion otherwise will point to Czechoslovakia, Poland, Norway and Cyrenaica – screaming at the incompetence of us soldiers and sheltering behind the delusions of his egotism.'

If one needs evidence of his strategical ability there is no finer example at this time than the famous Directive No. 21 outlining 'Barbarossa', his plan for the conquest of Russia –

where, he told Jodl, 'We have only to kick in the door and the whole rotten structure will come tumbling down'.

In its six pages – only nine copies were printed – the directive declares, first, that

'The German Armed Forces must be prepared to *crush Soviet Russia in a quick campaign* before the end of the war against England . . . Preparations are to be completed by 15th May 1941 . . . The mass of the Russian army in western Russia is to be destroyed in daring operations by driving forward deep armoured wedges, and the retreat of intact, battle-ready troops is to be prevented. The ultimate object of the operation is to establish a defence line against Asiatic Russia from a Line running from the Volga River to Archangel'.

Having stated the objective he went on to explain how attacks were to be launched in the north from Finland and in the south from Rumania. The dividing line between the two attacks would be the Pripet Marshes. One army group would gain possession of the Baltic States and Leningrad and another drive through White Russia and link up with it, trapping the Russian forces retreating from the Baltic. South of the marshes a third army group would advance through the Ukraine to Kiev. Their flank would be protected by Rumanian and German troops in the south who would move toward Odessa and the Black Sea and overrun the industrial concentration in the Donets basin.

It was all very skilful and practical. 'You have nothing to do but work out the details', he told Halder, 'and that you will do by the end of next month [January 1941]. It is vital that no delay should occur. There are vast distances to be dealt with in Russia and the Russian winter is also a deciding factor. The victory must be complete before we are called upon to fight the weather. All my plans are determined by that factor.'

So they may have been. He had not forgotten that both Charles XII and

The Sudeten crisis, 1938. *Above:* Chamberlain visits Hitler, 23rd September. *Left:* Hitler on 26th September: 'The Sudetenland is the last territorial claim I have to make in Europe.'

Napoleon had been defeated by the grim adversary Winter. But he had fatally left out of account another factor: his own irrepressible malice toward those who thwarted him.

The 'military missions' to Rumania of which the Russians were so justifiably suspicious, since the Rumanian frontier adjoins the Ukraine for some four hundred miles west from the Black Sea, had by the end of February 1941 been built into a force of nearly three quarters of a million men. Bulgaria, adjoining Rumania on the south, had also been inveigled into Hitler's grasp with the promise of access to the Aegean through an Axis-controlled Greece. The *quid pro quo* would be the occupation of Bulgaria by German troops and the consequent denial of Bulgaria to the British as a base from which they could bomb Rumanian oilfields.

Complete control of the Balkans, however, could not be gained without co-operation from Yugoslavia; and Prince Paul, who was ruling as Regent for the eighteen-year-old King Peter II, hurriedly and secretly trotted off with his Prime Minister and Foreign Minister to Vienna on 25th March as if they were obsequious puppies answering the bidding snap of the Führer's fingers. Without question they yielded to his demand that German troops and war material should be allowed transit through Yugoslavia, 'though those troops would at all times respect the sovreignty and territorial integrity of Yugoslavia'. Their prize, they were told, would be the Greek port of Salonika 'as soon as I have determined the Greek issue'.

Unfortunately for Hitler the Yugoslav people were not so anxious to sell out their country. While Paul was in Vienna their fury mounted and they prepared to overthrow the Regency

and bring young King Peter to the throne. Paul returned to find an uprising brewing. The Pact he and his Ministers had so obsequiously signed was in effect torn up. The German Ambassador, driving through the streets of Belgrade, was held up by a crowd celebrating the overthrow of the obnoxious régime of Hitler's puppet and the ambassadorial car was spat upon.

It was this insult even more than the ruination of his cunningly organized *coup* that infuriated Hitler. His malice manifested itself in a new military operation that was given first – and, as it turned out, fatal – priority. It was called, with singular lack of subtlety, 'Operation Punishment' and it was planned during and immediately after a meeting at the Chancellery on 27th March 1941 when Hitler was in such a rage that, according to Brauchitsch, 'there was froth on his lips and his clothes turned dark with sweat.' Brauchitsch and Halder attempted to calm him down and even went to the length of summoning the physician

Above: Dunkirk, May 1940. Evacuated troops take a last look. *Right:* Me-110s over London, August 1940

Morell. But he refused to be calmed. The Reich had been insulted by an intolerable insolence and there was no question of waiting to see if the young king's new government would come to heel as the Regent's had.

'Yugoslavia is to be crushed without mercy', he shouted. It was a repetition of the fist-banging display that Weizäcker had recorded in 1939 only much more violent. (The increasingly frequent rages and unrestrained violence were typical symptoms of the progress of syphilis.) 'No diplomatic enquiries will be made, no ultimatums will be presented. Yugoslavia will be mercilessly destroyed.'

At that stage Halder reminded him that he had ordered the start of 'Barbarossa' in mid-May – only six weeks hence – and that an additional task for the army of the magnitude of the complete destruction of a nation would inevitably delay it.

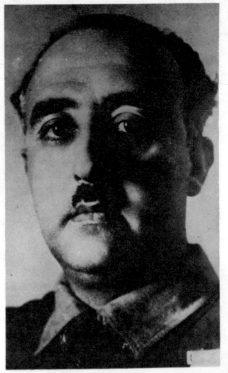

Above Left: Pierre Laval. *Above Right:* General Franco. *Right:* Battle of Sidi Birrani, January 1941. Some of Wavell's 150,000 Italian prisonners

'Only if I command a delay', Halder says Hitler told him.

'He was still raging and trembling. The General Staff stood rigidly in their places, fearing apoplexy . . . Morell stood helplessly by . . . Nobody could see the possibility of diverting forces for this new campaign; nor could we see the sense of expending so much on what was no more than a spiteful blow.'

It was that of course; but now that the justification for it had been given him it at once became more important – a stretching of his capacity. As Liddell Hart has said,

'The preparation and contemplation of vast strategic plans always intoxicated him. The doubts which his generals expressed, when he disclosed the trend of his mind, merely served to make it more definite. Had he not been proved right on each issue where they had doubted his capacity to succeed? He must prove them wrong again – and more strikingly. Their doubts showed that for all their subservience they still had an underlying distrust of him as an amateur'.

He did not in fact insist on maintaining the 'Barbarossa' schedule. Though his egomania might demand his refusal to appear to accept any orthodox military advice from his generals, he could hardly fail to be aware of his numerical inferiority in the matter of tanks compared with the Russians, or of the need for intensive concentrations of armour in the Balkans if he was to achieve quick conquest there. Therefore, on 1st April, when the General Staff were working out the details of the campaign in Yugoslavia, he commanded a postponement of the start of 'Barbarossa' from the middle of May to the middle of June.

So, on 6th April 'Operation Punishment' was launched. Belgrade war bombed to destruction by wave aftes wave of Göring's bombers. Nearly twenty thousand people were killed in that attack alone; and since the country was totally unprepared it surrendered within ten days.

At the same time, the German troops that had been massed in Bulgaria drove over the border into Greece, where Mussolini had met heroic resistance which time and again put his troops to flight. The Greeks had been reinforced by British divisions in March; but these too now were overcome by the huge forces that Hitler drove into the Balkans. (Twenty-eight divisions, including twenty-four that had been diverted from the 'Barbarossa' assembly area in Poland.) Only a week after Yugoslavia had been forced to capitulate Greece too was conquered; and by the end of April Hitler could – and did – taunt his generals with their apprehensions and point with triumph at

Left: General Erwin Rommel. *Above:*
Antonescu (right) the Rumanian Prime
Minister listens as his country is made a
German puppet state, December 1941

'two entire nations brought to heel
within a month in a campaign for
which no-one had the stomach'.

Nothing could have been more
potent fuel for his blazing megalomania. Metaphorically rubbing his
hands with the glee of the general for
whom no world is too great to conquer,
no campaign to complex, he ordered
the re-timed start of 'Barbarossa'.
The offensive was to begin at 0330 on
22nd June, and the codeword 'to set
Russia aflame and cause the world to
hold its breath' was 'Dortmund'.

Precisely on its scheduled hour
the codeword was given and the three
army groups began 'Barbarossa'. Two
hours later the German Ambassador
in Moscow called on Molotov and told
him Germany had decided to attack
Russia because too many Red Army
troops were in evidence along
the frontier and were threatening
Germany 'in defiance of the Pact of

22nd August 1939'. In Germany, at
seven o'clock, Goebbels broadcast the
Führer's proclamation, which in tone
was that of a shining Crusader in pur-
suit of a particularly noxious dragon:

'Weighted down with heavy cares,
condemned to months of silence, I
can at last speak freely. German
people! At this moment a march is
taking place that, for its extent,
compares with the greatest the world
has ever seen. I have decided again
today to place the fate and future of
the Reich and our people in the hands
of our soldiers. May God aid us,
especially in this fight.'

This nauseating bit of self-righteous
insolence was answered the same day
by Churchill in a broadcast that
edged round the difficult corners of a
policy that up to now had treated
Russia as hand-in-glove with Hitler
and therefore equally intolerable. It
too had its nauseous moments:

'The past, with its crimes, its follies,
its tragedies, flashes away. I see the
Russian soldiers standing on the
threshold of their native land, guarding the fields which their fathers have

Halder, Army Chief of Staff

tilled from time immemorial. I see them guarding their homes where mothers and wives pray – ah, yes, for there are times when all pray – for the safety of their loved ones, the return of the breadwinner, of their champion, their protector. I see the ten thousand villages of Russia . . . where there are still primordial human joys, where maidens laugh and children play'.

This roseate vision, though emotionally on key for the occasion for which it was written, like most of Churchill's speeches, was far from accurate. There were no Russian soldiers standing on the threshold guarding the tilled fields or the praying wives and mothers. 'The frontier guards, awakened by the squeal and clatter of tank tracks, were shot down as they emerged from their barracks, running half dressed through the smoke', says Alan Clark in *Barbarossa*. Aircraft were bombed to destruction as they stood on the airfields, as had happened in Poland. There was virtually no organized resistance against the tremendous impact of the initial invasion. For many days the Germans drove on into Russia almost unopposed. There were vast defensive forces but no plans. Heroic battles were reduced to mere skirmishes for lack of direction. Within a month Hitler's armies had

overrun three hundred miles on the whole of the thousand-mile front from Finland to the Black Sea.

On 3rd October he broadcast himself: 'I declare today – and I declare it without any reservation – that the enemy in the East has been struck down and will never rise again.'

It was characteristic of him that as soon as flaws appeared in the structure of his enterprises he plastered them over with the reassurances of a man pretending that unexpected events have been anticipated.

The first flaw had begun to appear in August. It was rather more than a hairline in the outer surface of the relationship between Hitler and the generals – always very thin ice. The problem, as always, was one of strategy – the generals clinging to the orthodox, Hitler to what he saw as bold and definitive.

Broadly, Hitler had determined on the plan outlined in the directive: in the north to clear the Baltic States and capture Leningrad with the aid of Army Group Centre; in the south to press toward Kiev and the Dniepr and lay hold of the vast resources of the Ukraine.

The generals, disturbed by the sudden stiffening resistance of the Red Army and the thinness of the German line caused by its excessive length, had different ideas. 'We have underestimated Russia', Halder reported on 17th August. 'We reckoned with 200 divisions and we have already identified 360. We have no depth in our offensive line and in consequence the enemy counter-attacks often meet with success.'

He and Brauchitsch pressed for a concentrated attack on Moscow. Hitler, however, would have none of it. 'He has rejected the Moscow plan', Halder wrote in his diary, 'and has decided that the strongest possible forces from Army Groups Centre and South are to be concentrated for a great pincer movement against the Soviet forces east of Kiev. The aim of defeating decisively the Russian

armies in front of Moscow has been subordinated to the desire to obtain the Ukraine . . . But the Führer has also now become obsessed with the idea of capturing both Leningrad and Stalingrad, for he has persuaded himself that if these two holy cities of Communism fall, Russia will collapse'.

The Kiev pincer movement was not completed until 20th September, by which time it was becoming clear that the blitzkrieg techniques that worked so well in the West quickly lost momentum in the vast steppes of Russia and eroded the German forces away in impossibly long lines of communication and difficulties of terrain. Hitler, however, drunk now with the false power of self-conviction, claimed in a scene of demonic triumph that his forces had won 'the greatest battle in the history of the world'. Halder dryly noted in his diary that in his opinion 'it was the greatest blunder of the Eastern campaign; for in the six weeks between the fall of Smolensk and the taking of Kiev the opportunity of seizing Moscow was lost.'

Since this was the point at which we

Brauchitsch (left) and Halder were unable, after 1940, to stand up to Hitler

see in retrospect the beginning of the end for Germany and the trail of Hitler's footsteps starting their rapid descent from the crest of power to the depths of ignominy, the moment is convenient to examine and label the seeds of defeat.

First and most disastrous was his insane determination to crush Yugoslavia without mercy and thereby delay the start of 'Barbarossa' by five fateful weeks. In his rage at Yugoslavia's refusal to acquiesce to the pact-signing grovelling of the puppet Regent, Hitler had deflected the course of action from that laid down in his own directive: 'The Russian winter is . . . a deciding factor. The victory must must be completed before we are called upon to fight the weather. All my plans are determined by that factor.' That was wise. But it was idiocy unbounded suddenly and solely for spite to increase a hundredfold the risk of encounter with the grim

Above: The Balkan Campaign, April 1941. A pontoon bridge hastily built over the River Vardar in Southern Yugoslavia. *Below:* Barbarossa. A supply column moves down a road in North Russia

Barbarossa. The pace slackens. *Above:* Exhausted infantrymen rest against a tank
Below: By October 1941 winter had begun. For the Germans the going became even tougher

Barbarossa assault

adversary of Napoleon, having already acknowledged the necessity of avoiding it.

Further delay had been caused by the profitless efforts of Halder and Brauchitsch, and the Army commanders, to persuade Hitler to change his mind. All in all, two months had been wasted.

There had been no misapprehension on Hitler's part regarding one side of the Russian character. 'The Russian will fight to the death on any given piece of ground; he will not yield it; you must destroy him.' But his contempt for their disorganization was to some extent misplaced. Lessons had been learned in Finland. The startling speed with which, once the tremendous advance into Russia had been made, the invaders were counterattacked was dangerously effective on such a wide front; and although some half a million Russians had been trapped in the Kiev pincers, plus another alleged half million in a subsequent encircling movement at Vyazama, the tremendous effort had wearied the Germans at the very moment when they needed fresh impetus to attack across terrain turned into a quagmire by early rains.

His obsessive determination to see Stalingrad and Leningrad fall cost him vast numbers of men and machines. Indeed the battle for Stalingrad proved to be the longest battle of the war – it lasted six months – and the complete end of the German Sixth Army; while the siege of Leningrad, during which countless thousands of Leningraders died of starvation, exhaustion and cold, yet held their beleaguered city against the enemy for nine hundred days, proved another facet of the Russian character that Hitler had underestimated – endurance. (The full stories of both cities in World War Two are told in *Stalingrad: The turning point* and *The Siege of Leningrad*, Battle Books 3 and 5 in this series.)

His contempt for his generals' judgement also, in the Eastern Campaign, reached maniacal proportions. The ludicrous result was that he gradually extended his insidious power downward until he literally could, and often did, control the movement of formations no larger than infantry platoons. Liddell Hart says that Rundstedt told him that toward the end of the war 'the only troops I was allowed to move were the guards in front of my own headquarters'.

The ambience of the daily 'conferences' he held is confirmed by many of the senior officers who gave evidence at the post-war Nuremberg trials. It was in every way similar to the imaginative constructions of those novelists given to building their melodramas round the efforts of power maniacs to gain control of the world.

'The reports of field commanders, collected and summarized by senior officers, would be given to him and he would direct the movement of this or that brigade or battalion, turning to the large-scale and highly detailed maps that were always the pictorial focal point of the conferences. His fantastic memory for detail often made him demand to know what had happened to, say, a particular machine-gun post. Why if its gunner had been killed, there had not been another at hand to take his place and "kill more enemy". When he was told once that "troops simply do not hold their ground when it's twenty-two degrees below zero" he gave orders that the post commander was to be shot immediately'.

His ravings were emphasized by bouts of uncontrollable twitching and sweating, moments when he was doubled up with obvious stomach pains, and an increasing tendency to wilful deafness when he was told of some indisputable fact that caught him momentarily at a loss to defend one of his own errors of judgement.

'Every midday conference became an absolute ordeal for the General Staff. The Führer would often either be screaming with frenzy or collapsing into a chair to become consumed with self-pity in which every reverse was caused by disloyalty or the weakness and stupidity of his allies. There were of course long spells of lucidity too, and in these his brilliance as a commander of every kind of formation was frequently evident. The trouble was, that in his position as supreme commander he should long ago have ceased to concern himself with the movement of patrols; but he could not bear to let control of anything pass from his hands. He was convinced he was superhuman and that the great destiny he served would transcend all perils and everything be brought to a triumphant conclusion.'

Triumphant conclusions were, as we know, far from the intention of his destiny; and avoidance of the *Tabes dorsalis* that forced him toward general paralysis of the insane was now impossible. *Tabes dorsalis* or *Locomotor ataxia*: syphilis involving the posterior columns of the spinal cord, is characterized by paroxysms, functional disorders of the stomach, inco-ordination of voluntary movements, and disturbances of vision. The infecting organism *Spirochaeta pallida* that had

enlarged his natural egotism into a state that grasped at, and to a great extent achieved, the absolute power of the megalomaniac, now had him in its absolute power. Lord Acton's gnomic dictum might be ironically adapted as 'All power corrupts and syphilitic power corrupts absolutely'.

Those, then, were the seeds of Hitler's and Germany's defeat. The generals had always been apprehensive about war on more than one front. Africa, the Balkans, the Atlantic, the Mediterranean – there was, as Westphal pointed out, a limit to the manpower and productive capacity of every nation. No-one could deny the Führer's skill in launching and carrying to success so much in so short a time. (The speed of that success had been largely due to the long and careful political preparation during the years 1919 to 1939.) No-one could deny either his almost visionary insight into the reactions of his opponents, military and political. But certainly no-one could deny his madness in refusing, as the Russian

Destroyed and abandoned German equipment lines a road outside Moscow

Left: Bormann, still in the side-lines at a Party-rally planning conference in 1934. *Above:* With Keitel and Hjtler at *Fuhrerhauptquartier* in 1941

campaign dragged wearily on, to accept any of the strategic plans of the men on the spot; for they were plans that could have ended, at best, only in negotiation or compromise. And nothing would have induced him to accept such a solution. As Chester Wilmot comments in *The Struggle for Europe*:

'He knew that neither his personal power nor that of the Nazi Reich would survive a settlement by negotiation. Having submitted the future of his régime, and of Germany, to the gamble of war, he had to continue to the last throw in the hope that the winning numbers would turn up. Total Victory or Total Defeat: that was the essence of the nihilist philosophy which was the foundation of Nazism.'

Dressed up, of course, it sounded like a brave man's clarion call. It was a call he had trumpeted a hundred times:

'I shall strike and not capitulate. The fate of the Reich depends on *me alone*. Every hope of compromise is childish. It is Victory or Defeat. The question is not the fate of a National-Socialist Germany, but who is to dominate Europe in the future. No one has ever achieved. what I have achieved. My life is of no importance in all this. I have led the German people to a great height, even if the world does hate us now. I am setting all my achievement on a gamble. I have to choose between victory and destruction. I choose victory. As long as I live I shall think only of the victory of my people. I shall shrink from nothing and destroy everyone who is opposed to me. I shall stand or fall in this struggle. I shall never survive the defeat of my people. There will be no capitulation to the powers outside, no revolution by the forces within.'

No: no-one could deny any of those things, those facts. The generals least of all. And perhaps many of them remembered the phrase 'I shall never survive the defeat of my people'. Hitler had said it to them in 1939.

The General in defeat

On the very day that Hitler was gloating over the signing of the Franco-German armistice in the railway car in the Forest of Compiègne – 22nd June 1940 – the first step was being taken to regain a British foothold on the continent of Europe. It was a faltering footstep; but it denied the validity of Hitler's promise that no Anglo-Saxon should ever land on the mainland again.

On the 23rd, at Churchill's instigation, a hundred commandos in a couple of boats – all that could be spared – made a raid on the French coast near Boulogne. Their object was to bring back prisoners and information about the coast defences there. They were unsuccessful; and indeed some of them, navigating themselves to the wrong port on their return journey, were ignominiously hauled ashore by the Military Police and arrested for desertion.

It was a brave if farcical beginning to the immense operation 'Overlord' that on 6th June 1944 brought the war in Europe to its final battles; but it

served to convince Churchill and the Army Command that though Britain was at that time helpless in terms of men and weapons sight must never be lost of the necessity for an eventual full-scale invasion. The conviction determined Churchill to form a Combined Operations Command whose task was to study and report on every possibility of achieving that object.

It was clear to anybody capable of making a simple statistical calculation that only the withdrawal of the bulk of the German occupation forces in north-west Europe could make an invasion possible. And at that time, with Hitler's men in gleeful possession of France and the Low Countries and German headquarters established triumphantly in fallen Paris, the likelihood of a withdrawal for any reason was, as the Chief of the Imperial General Staff recorded with

20th July 1944. Hitler, his hand bandaged, with Bormann, Jodl (bandaged head) and underlings soon after the bomb attempt

Joseph Stalin

masterly understatement, 'somewhat remote'.

Remote it remained, until precisely one year later and the start of 'Barbarossa'. The Battle of Britain and the increasing intensity of the Battle of the Atlantic fully occupied the attentions of the navy and the air force; and the army was desperately trying to overcome its decimation in France by training the thousands of conscripts who were gradually being drained from civilian life and for whom there seemed to be a permanent shortage of weapons and equipment. Then, with Russia betrayed in June 1941 – partly through her own greed and stupidity in allying herself with Germany – the balance of power shifted. It was a slight shift indeed: Hitler still kept fifty divisions defending northwest Europe and Norway. But it became evident as 'Barbarossa' progressed that the huge numbers needed to maintain the momentum of the invading forces must eventually be replenished from Europe or Africa.

Stalin, with a grizzling petulance discreditable in the leader of a great nation, did not fail to draw what he thought were the obvious deductions: that Britain should at once create a second front in Europe and so necessitate the return of some of the 150 German divisions engaged on the Eastern Front. His correspondence with Churchill at this time is full of accusations, appeals and demands. 'It was British failure in France that enabled Germany to invade the Ukraine . . . The Germans consider that England is merely bluffing, and they laugh at her cowardice while they transfer division after division to the East where our people spill their blood in defending our land against the growing might of the Nazis . . . Only when Britain opens a Second Front can we be assured of her friendship . . . How soon will aid come from Britain?'

With admirable restraint Churchill refrained from 'rubbing salt truths into the Russian wounds'. America, called by her President 'the great arsenal of democracy', had by that time under Lease-Lend begun supplying Britain with arms and armour, ships and ammunition. Many of these supplies, though sorely needed in the battles against Rommel in Africa and for equipping the expanding army in Britain were being diverted to Russia; and Churchill insistently maintained, with considerable patience and dignity in his replies to Stalin, that that was all that could be done for the moment – 'though I have already agreed with President Roosevelt that one of our principal aims should be to go to the aid of the conquered populations by landing armies of liberation when the opportunity is ripe'.

The opportunity was of course advanced by the Japanese attack on Pearl Harbor on 7th December 1941. At once America toppled over the brink of a neutrality sympathetic to Allied causes into unremitting war. Two weeks later Churchill, Roosevelt and George C Marshall (Chairman of the US Joint Chiefs of Staff) met in Washington and agreed on 'the strategic direction of all the forces of both nations, the allocation of manpower and munitions, the coordination of communications, the control of military intelligence, and the joint administration of captured areas'. It was also agreed that, 'notwithstanding the entry of Japan into the war, our view is that Germany is still the prime enemy and her defeat is the key to victory. Once Germany is defeated, the collapse of Italy and the defeat of Japan must follow.'

Firm words. And indeed their meaning and the consequent intention never wavered. But they were put somewhat awry by the lightning speed of events in the Far East. Singapore fell to the Japanese invaders on 15th February 1942 and there ensued a grave threat that the Axis powers might link up in the Indian Ocean, thus at one stroke isolating India, endangering Australasia, and leaving Russia's eastern seaboard vulnerable. To combat this threat it was necessary to divert the main Allied effort to halting the Japanese and safeguarding the Persian oilfields. No immediate concentration on the invasion of Europe was therefore possible.

There were in fact to be many more delays. These were caused mainly by the immense shipping losses in the Battle of the Atlantic, the continuing urgent demands by Russia for equipment for the desperate battles that raged month after month, and the incessant endeavour to build up the forces needed to defeat Rommel in the desert. Against these demands it was impossible to build up the equally necessary power to ensure success in a continental invasion. All the Chiefs of Staff were agreed that to attempt the invasion with inadequate forces would be to invite disaster. Stalin's petulance had turned to a somewhat threatening belligerence; and he secured from Roosevelt an unwisely

'The Anglo-Saxons'. Roosevelt and Churchill at their Atlantic meeting, August 1941. General Marshall on left

In the bag. General von Arnim surrenders to the British, Tunisia 1943

given undertaking that the Second Front invasion would be carried out in the second half of 1942. This communiqué was immediately qualified by Churchill in a note that said categorically 'It is impossible to say in advance whether the situation will be such as to make this operation feasible when the time comes. We can therefore give no promise in the matter.' But the Russians had already published the communiqué and for many months its promise proved embarrassing to the Allies and aroused considerable anger in Britain, where there was a characteristic feeling that promises should be honoured, not qualified.

Hitler, in his monstrous arrogance, appears to have convinced himself that so long as he kept up the war on shipping it would never be possible for the Allies to mount an invasion. In one of his frenzies he shouted at Field-Marshal Paulus, commander of the German Sixth Army in Russia, that 'neither England nor America singly or together can outdo me in military genius – and it is that, not mere numbers, that always decides victories'.

All the same, he spared no numbers in ordering a new offensive in the Stalingrad sector in October 1942 and another in the south. Both these came to grief by the massive counter-attack launched by Marshal Timoshenko on 19th November 1942. By 31st January 1943 Paulus had been forced to surrender. All available reinforcing German troops were sent forward from the Caucasus; but the Russians too had some strategic ability if not genius. The German move had been anticipated and the reinforcements were cornered. If 'Barbarossa' as a campaign had been the decisive point at which Hitler turned toward defeat, Timoshenko's counter-offensive was the pivot on which the ultimate German retreat was balanced. After it, battles flared up, offensives and counter-offensives were mounted, indifference into hopeless attacks and a few of these gained ground, or regained that which had been lost, for Hitler. But it had become apparent even to him that the tide had turned for the Allies. He may well have followed Clausewitz' dictum: 'He who uses force unsparingly without reference to the bloodshed involved, must obtain a superiority if his adversary uses less vigour in its application.' But his adversary in this case unexpectedly followed the same dictum – and used more vigour.

Also using more vigour – or more cunning strategy – was General Montgomery in Africa, his opponent-in-chief being General von Arnim, who had replaced Rommel in Tunisia. There the final battles in the African campaign raged until 12th May 1943, when Arnim surrendered. 'The North Africa Campaign had reached its conclusion', says Montgomery, 'and the remaining Axis survivors were lodged in captivity. It had ended in a major disaster for the Germans; all their remaining troops, equipment and stores were captured. Very few personnel were able to get away owing to. the effectiveness of the blockade by the Royal Navy and Royal Air Force which closed the escape routes by sea and air. It is idle to speculate why the Axis forces attempted to hold on in North Africa ... From a purely military point of view there was no justification for their action, but perhaps there were overriding political considerations.'

The 'political considerations' were no more than Hitler's involvement with his Axis partner, who had proved to be a broken reed. A much more insistent consideration was his own refusal to believe that anything he directed could possibly go wrong. Throughout the war his generals attempted to persuade him to surrender when surrender was justified – as it must sometimes be in war – and thereby gain advantage for the

The invasion of Italy. Salerno beach, September 1943

The invasion of France. A mass of US equipment on the beach, Normandy, June 1944

Above: Rundstedt, Commander in the West. Hitler undermined his authority by giving Rommel command of the troops in France, and then, on 1st July 1944, replaced him by Kluge
Left: General Kluge

future; and even more often they had tried to dissuade him from what seemed to them sheer madness in military tactics – as for example in his pretended intention to invade France immediately on the outbreak of war in 1939. In that and other cases they had been proved wrong and had reaped Hitler's taunts. His generalship had not been entirely undermined by his mania for individual power until he saw Russia within his grasp; and even then he might have come to conquest, or at any rate there might have been a very different outcome on the Eastern Front, if he had not allowed his vicious attack on Yugoslavia to delay the opening of 'Barbarossa' by those fateful five weeks.

As things were now, in 1943, he was soon to find his armies retreating on all fronts. The invasion of Sicily began on 10th July and was completed by 17th August. It was called by Montgomery, whose Eighth Army, together with the Seventh US Army carried out the operation, 'the first strike at the soft underbelly of the Axis in Europe'. It was a successful strike not only in a military sense but as a political move also Mussolini, brought time and again to impotent rage by his failure to influence Hitler, and to ignominy by the feeble performances of his swaggering, windfilled troops, was beside himself with fury at this new insult to Fascism. His son-in-law,

The scene at Rastenberg after the failure of Struffenberg's attempt. *Above:* Keitel, Göring, Hitler, and Bormann; Himmler behind. *Below:* The Duce is suitably moved by Hitler's escape

Count Ciano, says that he began to issue orders and counter-orders 'in a sequence that could lead only to certainty of his further inability to lead the country'. On 25th July, by which time the German defenders of the island had been forced back by the Seventh US Army to the north coast, the Italian dictator resigned and was immediately put under arrest by his successor, Marshal Badoglio. Badoglio entered into secret negotiations with the Allies and on 3rd September, when the Eighth Army was crossing the Messina Strait to land on the toe of Italy, signed an armistice treaty and agreed that it should be kept secret until Allied landings had been made at Salerno. The landings were made a few days later (on the 8th) and the news of the Italian capitulation broadcast.

Fortunately for Hitler the Allies did not follow up the Salerno landing either quickly or effectively – a failure for which the Supreme Commander, Eisenhower, later came in for considerable criticism. That failure allowed Hitler to demonstrate delaying action in Italy; indeed the final surrender of all German troops in Italy did not take place until 29th April 1945. But the delay did not alter the fact that once the Allies had secured their foothold in Sicily Hitler's armies were doomed – not least because that and earlier co-ordinated amphibious operations, of which the first was the tiny Commando raid of 22nd June 1940, had brought to the Combined Operations Command a wealth of experience that was to accumulate into the know-how for launching the greatest amphibious operation of all time – 'Overlord'.

At Soissons, only twenty miles east of Compiègne, there was an elaborate concrete bomb-proof shelter which Hitler had had built for his headquarters for the 'Sea Lion' operation in 1940. At nine o'clock on the morning of 17th June 1944 he arrived there for a meeting with his generals. Rommel and Rundstedt were there,

and the scene was recorded by General Hans Speidel:

'He looked pale and sleepless, playing nervously with his glasses and an array of coloured pencils which he held between his fingers. He sat hunched upon a stool, while the Field-Marshals stood. His hypnotic powers seemed to have waned. There was a curt and frosty greeting from him. Then in a loud voice he spoke bitterly of his displeasure at the success of the Allied landings, for which he tried to hold the field commanders responsible. The meeting lasted until four o'clock. At midday Hitler bolted a heaped plate of rice and vegetables after it had been previously tasted for him. Pills and liqueur glasses containing various medicines were ranged round his place and he took them in turn. Two SS men stood guard beside his chair.'

Everything here is indicative of the character of the man and the state of his health and mind. The crude ranting and transference of blame from his own shoulders to those of the professionals he hated; the hypochondria; the fear that comes to all megalomaniacs that brooding conspiracies exist (it was a well grounded fear, as we shall see); and the obvious, if temporary, implicit inability to deal with an overwhelming situation. The situation did indeed demand rather more than the attention of a sick syphilitic verging on the borders of lunacy.

At 6.30 am on 6th June the first wave of five invading British and American divisions, carried in 4,266 ships and landing craft, had landed on the Normandy beaches. They had been preceded, at 2am, by more than 3,000 aircraft carrying airborne troops; an aerial bombardment from 2,219 bombers starting at 3.14am; and a naval bombardment at 5.50am. Convoying and covering the landings was a total of 702 warships and 25 flotillas of minesweepers; and in the air a total of 171 squadrons had prepared the way before D-day by

attacking railways, bridges and aerodromes. This immense force was under the Supreme Command of General Dwight Eisenhower.

In terms of men on the ground opposing it there was a much mightier force: fifty infantry and ten panzer divisions. But these of course covered a huge area – Normandy, Brittany, the Pas de Calais, Flanders, Holland, the Biscay coast and the Riviera. In Normandy were nine infantry divisions and one Panzer division. In charge and directing this defensive force – as much as any of Hitler's generals could ever be said to be directing anything – was Field-Marshal von Rundstedt, Commander-in-Chief in the West. But because he had expressed the view to Hitler that France should be evacuated and its garrison withdrawn to the German frontier, in preparation for the Allied invasion that was obviously being planned, Hitler had humiliated him by giving ostensible command of all troops in France to Field-Marshal Rommel. 'In this way', General Speidel says, 'he maliciously set the two Field-Marshals against each other, knowing that even in the *method* of defending France they had divergent views. Thus they would have to rely on him for the solution, thereby emphasizing their reliance on him.'

Having been forced to accept the decision that there would be no withdrawal to the German frontier, Rundstedt held that if France were to be defended the best method was to keep the main body of the army well back from the coast, allow the Allied force to gain a foothold, and then attack from well in the rear of the coastal defences with such power that would drive the enemy back into the sea. Rommel was all for destroying the enemy as he landed, for which he

Above: **Destruction in the Falaise pocket.**
Left: **The Ardennes counterattack.**
Germans advance past abandoned US
vehicles. December 1944

1925

1926

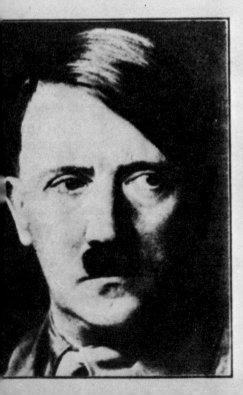

1927 **1928**

would naturally demand extremely strong beach garrisons backed by solidly packed reserves no more than a few miles from the coast.

The solution as given by Hitler – a fatal one – was a compromise. It was not, on the face of things, an unreasonable one. The infantry were to be kept well forward and the mechanized forces in the rear. But compromises are rarely satisfactory in desperate times; and this occasion proved to be no exception to the rule. The fact that the great warlord was supposedly directing the entire enter-prise from his eyrie in Wolfeschanz was of no help to anybody; while his maniacal order that no reserves were to be thrown into the battle without his personal approval was a hindrance that had disastrous consequences.

However, in one of his latterly rare flashes of psychological insight he proved his generalship once again, and almost for the last time – that last time was to be in the Ardennes in the coming winter – by assessing correctly the point at which the invasion would be made. Rundstedt had supposed the invasion fleet would land at the

narrowest part of the English Channel, between Calais and Dieppe, that being the method that hidebound strategy would dictate; but Hitler, according to General Warlimont, who was on his staff, did not think that Eisenhower – in no sense an orthodox general – would concede anything to orthodoxy. It was much more probable, Hitler said, that the landing – 'if it isn't all a gigantic bluff' – would take place between Caen and Cherbourg, 'because they will need a big port, and what other is there?' Rommel accordingly tightened up his

Nuremberg, scene of Hitler's triumphs, falls to the Americans, April 1945

defences in the Normandy area.

But to be right in a psychological appreciation is of little use if one is to be wildly wrong in the administration of the steps taken to meet it. To act the puppet master in a remote lair in Berchtesgaden and then to restrict one's generals in their executive power is to court disaster.

The first of the disastrous consequences occurred before D-day. Rommel had only one Panzer division

in Normandy, and this he had positioned at Caen. Having come round – indeed not having much choice – to Hitler's viewpoint on the place of the expected landings he had asked for another Panzer division to place near St Lô – where in fact it would have been of great value in dealing with the Americans. But he was refused. Hitler having compromised on the method of defence was determined to keep his armour to the rear, and the nearest available additional armour was some miles to the north-west of Paris. This bothered Rommel so much that he determined to make a trip to Hitler's headquarters to try to persuade him. Since Hitler had forbidden his commanders to travel by air because of the activities of the Royal Air Force, Rommel made the trip by road on 5th June. He had been assured by the meteorological report that high winds and rough seas made any kind of invasion extremely unlikely. (Eisenhower had actually postponed D-day from 5th June to 6th June for that very reason.) He therefore drove first to his home near Ulm to greet his wife on her birthday and stayed with her that night. When, on the morning of the 6th he set out for Berchtesgaden the invasion had already begun.

It was therefore Rundstedt's headquarters that telephoned Hitler at 4am, as soon as the airborne landings made it virtually certain that the invasion was about to begin. They received a dusty answer. Hitler was still in bed and Jodl dared not wake him. He categorically refused to release the reserve Panzer Corps. He was certain that the Normandy landings were no more than a feint and that in a short while there would be a full-scale landing east of the Seine – 'when the reserve Panzer Corps will serve the proper purpose the Führer has decided for it'.

Meanwhile, as plea after plea was made and refused, the Americans had

Soviet bombers over Berlin, April 1945

A dishevelled-looking Führer inspects Hitler Youth members in the garden of the Reich Chancellery. Taken late in March 1945, and one of the last pictures of Hitler

got a footing on two beaches and the British on one and in parts had penetrated inland for five miles. From then on the invasion was scarcely ever to be checked.

It was scarcely surprising, therefore, that on the morning of 17th June Hitler should speak bitterly 'of his displeasure at the success of the Allied landings'. By that time the advance had secured the link-up of all the beach-heads into a continuous front. 400,000 men, 60,000 vehicles, and 100,000 tons of stores had been landed. The prefabricated ports called 'Mulberries' had been towed across the Channel and built and the 'Pluto' (Pipe Line Under The Ocean) continuous oil supply laid. Air mastery was absolute. 'In fine weather', says Eisenhower, 'all enemy movement was brought to a standstill by day.'

Blind to the hopelessness of the situation, which Rundstedt and Rommel attempted to reveal to him, Hitler did nothing but shriek 'There must be no withdrawal! You must stay where you are!' Rundstedt adds: 'He would not even agree to allow us any more freedom than before in

where the Allies and their supplies continued to pour in. Needless to say, the implied criticism did nothing but arouse a towering rage in the Führer. The only thing that calmed him was a suggestion by Rommel that he should visit the Normandy battlefield and personally inspire the troops to die where they stood rather than withdraw. This he agreed to do two days hence, on the 19th.

He never made the visit. Early in the evening of the 17th, when the 'conference' with the generals had ended and Hitler was being driven to Compiègne, where presumably he intended to make some symbolic genuflection or draw some kind of inspiration, a V1 on its way to London cut its engine and fell with destructive force on the Soissons bomb shelter. No-one was hurt, but Hitler was so alarmed by his narrow escape that he turned tail and drove back to Berchtesgaden with all speed. It was an echo of his speedy disappearance from the scene of the *putsch* of 9th November 1923.

On 20th June a violent new offensive by the Russians began. It destroyed all German resistance in its path and in two weeks the eastern border of Poland had been crossed and East Prussia itself was in danger. There was nothing to be done except withdraw reinforcements from the Western Front – hardly helpful in stemming the invasion tide there. Nor was it any solution to get rid of Rundstedt – which Hitler did on 1st July because Rundstedt had expressed 'defeatist views' – and replace him by Field-Marshal von Kluge.

Nothing whatever, in fact, could now alter the course of defeat except a miracle. Hitler's generals did not believe in miracles any more than they now believed in the Führer's ability to lead Germany anywhere but into utter destruction. Though he had inspired violent personal hatred in many of the professionals for whom he had shown such contempt it was, to do them justice, not so

moving the forces as we thought best. As he would not modify his orders, the troops had to continue clinging on to their cracking line. There was no plan any longer. We were merely trying, without hope, to comply with Hitler's order that the line Caen-Avranches must be held at all costs.'

The only compensation he offered the generals was the new weapon, the V1 Flying Bomb, 'which it is certain will have a decisive effect on the war if, as I intend, it is directed exclusively on London so as to bring the English to the idea of peace'. Speidel says the two field-marshals then ironically suggested that there would be more sense in directing it on to the beaches much that hatred as a wish to end the war honourably for Germany on which they based the conspiracy to kill him.

The conspiracy involved a great many people; but the actual planting of the bomb under the table in the Führer's headquarters on 20th July 1944 was done by Lieutenant-Colonel Count Klaus Schenk von Stauffenberg. Unfortunately the bomb failed to do more than inflict superficial injuries on Hitler and inspire him to tell Mussolini, whom he met an hour or so later, that divine providence had been at work again and that his life had been saved so that he in turn could save the German nation. But it led to a paralysis of fear infecting the High Command in the weeks and months that followed, for Himmler's Gestapo ruthlessly sought out all who had, or might have had, even the most tenuous association with the plot. Among them was Kluge, whose name had been found mentioned in papers revealed by the Gestapo investigation.

'All this', says Liddell Hart in *The Other Side of the Hill*, 'had a very bad effect on any chance that remained of preventing the Allies from breaking out [of the Avranches-Caen front]. In the days of crisis Field-Marshal von Kluge gave only part of his attention to what was happening at the front. He was looking back over his shoulder anxiously – toward Hitler's headquarters.'

A few days later all that was left of the defensive German armies on the Western Front became trapped in the 'Falaise Pocket'. Kluge was sacked. He committed suicide by taking a poison tablet. But it was not the humiliation of being relieved of his command that brought him to self-destruction: he had supposed – with every justification – that he would be arrested by the Gestapo within a few hours.

On 29th July General Patton's Third American Army crossed the Seine. General Eisenhower reported

that no effective barrier now lay between him and Brittany, for the enemy was in a state of complete disorganization. The invasion, as such, was over. According to Major-General J F C Fuller, 'final victory was assured irrespective of what happened on any other front. Yet it was more than a victory: it was a revolution which cracked the age-old foundations of maritime security. Conclusively, it showed that, granted the necessary industrial and technical resources, no coastline, whether of a continental or an insular power, even when strongly defended, was henceforth secure. It proved that, had Hitler allotted but a fraction of the

resources at his disposal between the years 1933 and 1939 to solving the problem of the English Channel, he would have won the war.'

Final victory may well have been assured. But there was still plenty of time for the perpetration of mistakes. And most of them, as it happened, were on the Allies' side. The advance toward Germany was harried by curious organizational failures, not least of which was a shortage of petrol. And in the interval, which was accounted for by the euphemistic phrase 'refitting, refuelling and rest', the Germans had got together a few weak divisions and some astonishingly active and courageous parachutists

Victorious Russians parade in the shattered streets of Berlin

who inflicted considerable damage in spite of their small numbers. That limited delay led to a longer one during which a fairly stout resistance was built up along the Rhine front. It was a case of differing ideas of strategy held by General Montgomery and Generals Bradley and Patton on the American side. Eisenhower was naturally unwilling to approve outright the strategy of either the English or American leaders and again, with just as dire results as Hitler had reaped, compromise was resorted to. Here was a clash of

personalities that was never truly resolved, as was to be seen in the post-war memoirs of the generals concerned; and it is difficult to see what else Eisenhower could have done in the circumstances. He had become what Liddell Hart called 'the rope in a tug of war between his chief executives'.

All the same, however much blame may or may not be attached to personal antagonism in high places, the most deep-seated cause of the Allies' failure to complete their victory in September 1944 was a kind of ennui, an unjustifiably optimistic attitude of 'uh-huh! We've won the war; let's relax'. It seemed to permeate the ranks from top to bottom; and its influence reached Hitler in the form of one of his intuitive flashes of psychological insight. It was the last; but in his dying mind it inspired the boldest counterstroke of all.

On the morning of 16th December, a day after Montgomery had sent Eisenhower a cheque for £5 to settle a bet that the war would be ended by Christmas, a huge – huge considering Hitler's desperate circumstances – offensive was launched in the beautiful, hilly, wooded country of the Ardennes. This was precisely where he had launched his break-through in the spring of 1940, and it is almost unbelievable that the Allies, with everything in the history of the Second World War to prove them wrong, had ridiculously left that gate open once again – and for the same reason that France had left it open earlier: because it was considered unsuitable country for the movement of armour.

That it wasn't unsuitable was again made quickly evident. Hitler had assembled, from all he had been able to gather of his remaining tanks, plus all that had been got into production during October and November,

a new Sixth Panzer Army. Against this, stretched sparsely across the Ardennes front, were a mere four divisions. These were quickly penetrated by seven armoured and thirteen other divisions of the Sixth Panzer Army, with devastating effect. In addition, chaos was caused in the Allied lines by German commandos who, disguised in American uniforms and riding in captured American jeeps, cut communications, turned signposts, put down notices indicating non-existent minefields, and in general adapted to confusing use the technique of the Trojan Horse.

Eisenhower says that when the news of the counter-attack reached him at his headquarters at Versailles late in the afternoon of the 16th he 'was immediately convinced that this was no local attack', and he immediately alerted the two divisions he held in reserve at his headquarters. But their arrival on the scene was too late to stem the attack. Consequently the final collapse of the Reich was delayed for a little under five months – and at very great cost to the Allies, particularly the Americans, who bore the brunt of the counter-attack.

Not that the Ardennes campaign itself lasted for five months – or indeed anything like. By Christmas day Patton's Third Army had knocked the stuffing out of Sixth Panzer Army and Hitler was once more indulging in wishful thinking. 'A tremendous easing of the situation has come about', he told Rundstedt (who by that time had been reinstated in command). 'The enemy has had to abandon all his plans for attack. He has been obliged to regroup his forces. He has had to throw in again units that are tired. And at home he is being criticized and is having to admit that there is no chance of the war being decided before next August, perhaps not before the end of next year.'

Wishful thinking indeed. By 1st January Rundstedt's forces were in full retreat and by the end of

Above: This 1934 portrait shows
Hitler's fondness for dogs and the
bourgeois vulgarity of his taste. *Right:*
Posing with coalminers in the thirties

the month the total German losses
amounted to some 70,000 casualties in
men plus 50,000 prisoners, 600 tanks,
nearly 2,000 aircraft, and countless
vehicles. The Führer's intuition had
resulted in a brilliant plan; but just
as he had always built his personal
power into impossible realms of
control, so had he grossly over-
estimated his own military strength.
And though it took the Allies far
longer to recover from the shock of
his impact in the Ardennes than it
should have done, it still remained
true that final victory had been
assured when Patton's Army had
crossed the Seine and 'Overlord'
was completed.

The collapse of the Sixth Panzer
Army caused an immediate benefit
to the Russians, for on the Eastern
Front nothing could be done to keep

their armies from advancing. And, as Major-General Fuller says, in any sane war 'hostilities would have been brought to an immediate end [after the Ardennes offensive]. But because of unconditional surrender the war was far from being sane. Gagged by this idotic slogan, the Western Allies could offer no terms, however severe. Conversely, their enemy could ask for none, however submissive. So it came about that, like Samson, Hitler was left to pull down the edifice of Central Europe upon himself, his people and their enemies. The war having been irretrievably lost, chaos was now his political aim, and thanks to unconditional surrender he was in a position to achieve it.' The struggle for domination of eastern and western powers since the war is another story; but in setting in motion that struggle Hitler may be said to have achieved his aim. Which no doubt would have pleased him.

The war as a military exercise continued now in predictable leaps and bounds. Cologne was captured on 7th March, Frankfurt on the 29th, Nuremberg – where so much Nazi doctrine had been spouted and so many millions fell under the spell of Hitler's 'hypnotic personality' – on 20th April. On the 29th all German troops in Italy laid down their arms. Almost at the same moment Hitler was signing his last will in the Chancellery in Berlin while the Red Army encircled the city. It was a blindly furious document in which he attacked Jews, traitors, capitalists – even Himmler and Göring, who, he said, had betrayed him to the Allies and shamed the German nation. He denounced all who had accused him of war or warlike aims, and in what he presumably thought to be a dignified farewell, to a deeply concerned world, added:

'I cannot forsake the city which is the capital of this state. Since our forces are too small to withstand any

Hitler's public encounters with children were stage managed and publicised with great skill

longer the enemy's attack on this place, and since our own resistance will be gradually worn down by an army of blind automata, I wish to share the fate that millions of others have accepted and to remain here in the city. Further, I will not fall into the hands of an enemy who requires a new spectacle, exhibited by the Jews, to divert hysterical masses.' (On the previous day Mussolini had been caught and executed by Italian partisans while attempting to escape to Switzerland, and his body had been exhibited to public insult.) 'I have therefore decided to remain in Berlin and there to choose death voluntarily at the moment when I believe that the residence of the Führer can no longer be held.'

A few hours earlier Hitler had married his mistress, Eva Braun, in a bizarre ceremony in the bunker below the Chancellery. On the following day,

30th April, at 3.30 in the afternoon, Hitler took a revolver and shot himself through the mouth, and either immediately before or immediately after that suicidal shot Eva Braun swallowed poison. Hitler's body was wrapped in a blanket by Heinz Linge, his valet, and together with that of Eva Braun was soaked in petrol and burnt in the Chancellery garden. 'The sight of Hitler's shattered head', said one of the Chancellery guards who witnessed the funeral pyre, 'was repulsive in the extreme.'

It was a suitably Wagnerian end to a man who believed himself to be the saviour of the German race; and no doubt had it been possible the cremation would have been accompanied by the music of *The Entry of the Gods into Valhalla*. But nothing except the sound of Russian shells bursting was to be heard. The Gethsemane of Adolf Hitler – Führer, 'noble wolf' and 'protector of the Gentiles' – was aflame amidst the forces he had loosed upon the world and upon himself.

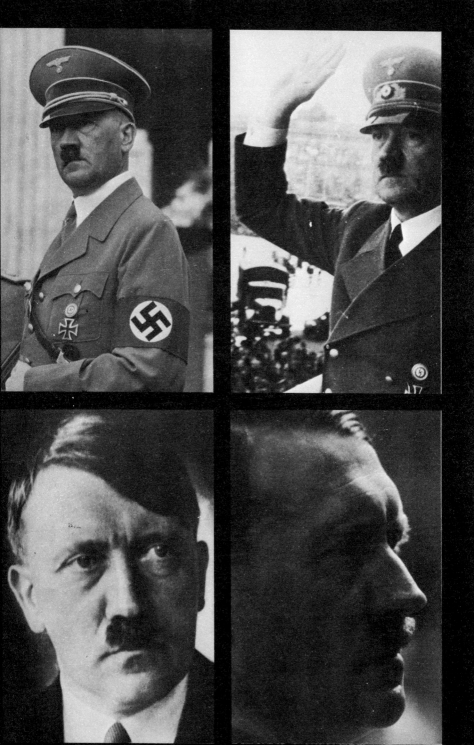

Bibliography

Hitler by Konrad Heiden (Constable)
The Last Days of Hitler by H R Trevor-Roper (Macmillan, London & USA)
Hitler's Interpreter by Paul Schmidt (Heinemann, London)
The Ciano Diaries by Count Galeazzo Ciano (Heinemann, London. Fetig, USA)
Hitler's War Directives by H R Trevor-Roper (Sidgwick & Jackson, Pan Books, London)
Inside Hitler's Headquarters by Walter Warlimont (Weidenfeld & Nicholson, London. Praeger, USA)
Hitler as War Lord by Franz Halder (Putnam)
Berlin Diary by William Shirer (Hamish Hamilton)
The Rise & Fall of the Third Reich by William Shirer (Secker & Warburg, London. S & S, USA)
The Limits of Hitler's Power by Edward N Peterson (Princeton University Press USA)
The Speeches of Adolf Hitler (Oxford University Press. Fertig, USA)
Hitler by Alan Bullock (Odhams, London. Harper-Row, USA)